The Past ... or the Coming Future

The Past ...
or the Coming Future

By
L.C. Walker

A Leathers Publishing Production
4500 College Blvd.
Leawood, KS 66211
Phone: 1 / 888 / 888-7696

Copyright 1998
Printed in the United States

ISBN: 1-890622-32-X

A Leathers Publishing Production
4500 College Blvd.
Leawood, KS 66211
Phone: 1 / 888 / 888-7696

DEDICATION

To fellow believers in Christ who are looking forward to the rapture of the Church and want to share this Blessed Hope with their friends and relatives.

FOREWORD

Many people want to know what is going to happen in the future.

The Bible outlines the events which will take place in the near future. Those future events spoken of in the book of The Revelation and those in Daniel will be fulfilled during the tribulation. We know there is no other prophecy that has to be fulfilled in order for Christ to rapture his Church. God wants everyone to be with him in heaven some day. However, some will choose not to be with Him.

This book describes events prior to and the 45 days following the rapture. My book is based on how I believe the world is being prepared for the coming tribulation. My guide was the Bible. I tried to stay as close to the Word as possible.

The characters in this book and the dates are fictitious. No one knows the hour or the day when Christ will return for His children. Hopefully, you will enjoy reading this book and it will help you to prepare for that glorious day — the day the Church is RAPTURED!

PROLOGUE

A trumpet sounded all through heaven and everyone knew what it meant. All of the immortals from the church age are supposed to appear at the Gathering Place. Once we were all there, Christ made his proclamation:

"It is now time for you to teach about the times prior to the rapture and the seven-year tribulation. I am lifting the ban I imposed 300 years ago. You must tell them how the world was being prepared by the Antichrist and the False Prophet. Tell about the rapture and the 45-day lull period. When you start to tell them of the tribulation, I want you to let them know how bad it was on earth during that period of cruelty.

Remember, all the people who were alive at the start of the millennium were saved. They made it completely through the worst period in the history of the world. Many have been born since that time. They still have a choice to make during My Millennial reign as to whom they will accept. No matter where they are, when the Devil is let out of the pit, I don't want any person to say they have never heard the story and they never had a chance to accept Me as their personal Savior. It is your job to tell them of that time and what they must do to be saved so they can enter the New Heavens and the New Earth which God, the Father, the Holy Spirit, and I will create."

CHAPTER 1

THE DAY BEGAN just like any other day, but this day was going to be a very special day, a day that would be spoken of for hundreds of years to come. The topic I was going to speak about had not been spoken of for almost 300 years. As a matter of fact, it had been forbidden to even mention this topic. On this day, June 23, 2387, all teachers were allowed to teach and answer any questions that might be asked concerning this topic.

As I started my descent to earth, I knew there would be so many questions it would take more time than I had figured, but what was time? The people on earth had plenty of time. They would have another 600 years to think about what I was going to say.

I remembered how the world was before the tribulation began. I remembered the day the trumpet sounded and all Christians were caught up in the air to meet the LORD. That was the second greatest day of my life. The greatest was the day I became a Christian. The descent only took seconds, so I didn't really have a lot of time to think about the past, but that would change today. This day, I would tell about the past.

It was 7:00 in the morning, earth time, and a very cool day for June, but with the canopy around the world it kept the mornings cool and damp. Even though I could not be seen yet, I could see all of the people on the lawn, and within seconds I would become visible to them. My thoughts raced through my mind while I stood there waiting for the talking to stop and I could begin. No one in the crowd knew we had been given permission by the LORD to talk about the years just prior to the rapture and what had occurred during the tribulation.

The people who became Christians during the tribulation and made it all the way through the seven years talked about how bad it was during that time. They had children, and their children had children, and so on until now. About 60 years into the millennium, the parents stopped telling the new generations how terrible the tribulation was and how millions of people died for their faith in Jesus Christ. Jesus said, "Since the parents do not want to tell the new generations about the tribulation, the subject is forbidden to be spoken of until one day in the coming future." Almost 300 years have passed, and now the LORD said, "It is time to remember what happened in the tribulation and never to forget, unless they let history repeat itself."

My group of followers, that make up the township of Clearmount, is small in number compared to other towns the immortals are responsible for. I started with a mere 44 people. The 44 turned into 100, then 200, and now there are so many I can hardly remember all the names. I really do enjoy teaching, no matter how small or how large the group may get. The 44 people who started this small community in 2018 is the largest community within 200 miles.

When the LORD put the canopy around the world, the way it was before the flood, the population of the world started to sky-rocket. One of the main reasons why the population sky-rocketed was because the harmful sun's rays that cause cancer could not penetrate the canopy. Everyone who made it through the tribulation is almost 400 years old or older. I can only remember a few deaths since the canopy went around the earth, and that was because of sin. The Bible says people can live to be 1,000 years old in the millennium.

I decided I would start telling the group about my life, how I was saved, and then tell about the events that led up to the rapture. I also wanted to tell them of Tom and Debbie Hale's life during the tribulation.

Tom and Debbie were such great people, I could use no better examples to show the love of Christ. Also, with Tom being 92 years old when the tribulation began and Debbie being 93, it was a miracle they made it through the tribulation without dying. I guess you could say Tom and Debbie were two of the very first believers after the rapture. Their two sons, two daughters, 14 grandchildren, and all their great-grandchildren had already accepted Christ as their Savior prior to the rapture. Tom and Debbie did not believe there was going to be a rapture or a tribulation or a man called the Antichrist.

Tom's oldest son, Charlie, had gone to a youth rally at the age of 14 and believed what he heard and became a Christian. Charlie told his brother Sam, who was two years younger than he was. The next day at the next rally, Sam also became a Christian. Charlie, being the oldest, always felt he should be the one to set the example. If he did something he thought was right, he would talk Sam, Connie, and Candy into it also. When he became a Christian, he knew the others should become Christians also, and they did. He told his parents, Tom and Debbie, about Christ and how He died for the sins of the world and how they needed a Savior. Charlie never could talk Tom and Debbie into becoming Christians. Charlie showed them all the predictions of Christ's first coming — even though it appeared they were not listening — and what the Bible said about his second coming, but Tom and Debbie would not believe, until that one day in February.

On February 17, 2011, all of those beliefs came to a sudden halt. Tom and Debbie were celebrating their 70th wedding anniversary with all of their family members, when everyone disappeared. There was no one left except them. They knew exactly what had happened because of what Charlie had told them about the rapture. Before the day was over, they were on their knees asking for forgiveness and asking Christ to come into their hearts. Tom told Debbie he wished he would have listened to what Charlie was saying, instead of letting it go in one ear and out the other. Before this time Tom had questioned, "What does a teenage boy know?"

Tom and Debbie were too busy to listen to things about God and the Bible. They both believed there was a God, but to have a personal relationship with him and to know that he was Jesus Christ, the only Savior for the world, was incomprehensible to them.

They knew things were going to get worse from this point on. They also knew from what Charlie had said, that 45 days after the rapture, the tribulation would begin. They had to tell as many people as would listen to them, that the day had come that the Bible had predicted. How many people would listen, and how many people would think they were crazy, no one knew. It did not make any difference, they had to tell as many as would listen. If only a handful of people believed, they might tell their friends and just maybe it would start to snowball, and many, many people would accept Christ before it was eternally too late.

Many preachers taught that if anyone heard the gospel before the rapture, during the tribulation, they could not and would not accept Christ as their Savior. That was true to a point. Those people who were in church and heard the gospel every Sunday and knew they had to accept, but chose not to, would not accept Christ in the tribulation.

Tom and Debbie had no idea how many souls would come to Christ because of them. Sometimes it was just a word or just an act of kindness that changed people's hearts. Some people said they had lost their minds and it was just a matter of time before they would die of old age. I guess those people were really fooled. Tom and Debbie made some decisions that changed people's lives forever.

Living in the same house with the Antichrist and almost going completely through the tribulation without him knowing they were Christians was a miracle. The results of food and water Tom gave to people who were starving and dying from thirst could not be measured. He always gave a little tract about Christ and how a person could become a Christian. Most of the people he never saw again. But that little bit of kindness was all it took for people to accept. Tom and Debbie knew if they were caught giving food or water to anyone who had not taken the number, 666, they would be executed immediately. It did not make any difference, they would die for Christ. Many, many times they were so close to being caught they figured it was their time to die. But the Lord had other plans; they would make it through the tribulation and they would bring a multitude to a saving knowledge of Christ.

I've had plenty of time to think about what I will share with everyone. I am not going to leave anything out; I am going to tell the whole story. Even though I am going to start with my life, I am going to focus more on the things that happened before the rapture and during the 45-day lull period. Then I will tell the people of the things that happened in the tribulation. I want to tell them about the Antichrist and the False Prophet. Also they need to know about the falling away and the setting up of the false religion.

Now that the talking has died down I can now begin to tell everyone how it was before the rapture. I know as I tell about the past, memories will come back to those who went through the tribulation, and there may be some tears as they think back. If those who took the number of the Antichrist could hear me teaching about the past, they would be wishing they had a second chance, but it is not so. They had their chance and they refused to accept Christ. The things I am going to tell should make everyone thank the LORD for what he did over 2,400 years ago on the cross. As I look around, I wonder to myself, how many of these people will be in that number that will reject Christ at the end of the millennium, when the devil is let loose for a little while?

THE LIFE OF PROFESSOR STEVEN L. WILSON

CHAPTER 2

THE BREEZE WAS COOL on my face as if we had just had a spring shower. I thought back to when I was a small boy, how I loved the rain, and the smell in the springtime. I wondered if the people in this community ever thought about the simple things that Jesus provided daily, or did they just take them for granted? I motioned with my hands to ease it down so I could start my teaching session.

The outside theater, in which we were seated, was built almost 200 years ago. The theater could seat 144,000 people. The way the theater was constructed, the speaker could be heard from any seat, without shouting. The most memorable time this small group recalled was the time when Christ came to speak. The people were spellbound. They did not know what to say or what to do when Christ was finished. They sat there amazed that GOD would come to their small town and speak. Every year, everyone was required to go to Jerusalem for the worship of Christ at the temple, but for Christ to come here was a real honor. Now I would begin my teaching session from that same platform.

"I want to take you back to the time just before I became a Christian. I was born May 9, 1957, in a small town in Oklahoma by the name of Perry. Perry was just about an hour north of Oklahoma City. After high school, I went to Oklahoma University where I received my degree in Chemical Engineering. In 1979, I went to work for Union Petroleum. My job was to look for places where the company might drill for oil. I usually worked in southern Oklahoma and Northern Texas. One day in mid-April, I was working in the Turner Falls area, when I was bitten by a diamond-back rattlesnake. I was rushed to the hospital, given anti-venom serum, which I did not know I was allergic to, and almost died. I was told that I was in a coma for almost three days. I remember opening my eyes once to see a beautiful blonde woman in white standing over me. I thought I was in heaven. I later found out it was one of the nurses.

"After I came out of the coma, I guess I did what everyone who comes close to death does; they say they will do anything if God will heal them. When I made that statement, I really did mean what I said. I asked one of my friends, who had witnessed to me previously, and I knew was a Christian, if he would have his pastor come see me and tell me what I must do to be saved. The next day my friend's pastor came to my room. I explained to him that I wanted to be saved.

"First, he told me I was a sinner and in order to be a Christian, I must admit I was a sinner.

"Second, he said I must believe Christ died on the cross for my sins.

"Third, I must believe Christ was buried and rose again the third day, and finally I must ask Christ to come into my heart.

"The pastor directed me to John 3:14-18. I told the Lord I was a sinner and I wanted forgiveness of my sins. By faith, I believed what the Bible said. The pastor led me in a prayer, and I accepted Christ as my personal Savior. After that day, I began to read my Bible daily, and I also started going to church. I was not going to back down from the oath I had taken on my death bed.

"I worked another four months for Union Petroleum, and at the beginning of the school year I enrolled at Dallas Theological Seminary, majoring in Greek and Hebrew. I had no idea what the Lord had planned for my life, but wherever He would lead me, that is where I would go.

"In 1984 I received my master's degree in Greek and Hebrew. The seminary asked if I would be interested in teaching there and I said I would love to. While I worked as a professor, I was also working on my doctorate. In 1986, I was married and I also received my doctorate in Hebrew. I did not know everything that had happened to me up to this point in my life was setting me up for what would happen later in my life.

"My wife Joan and I had three children, two boys and a girl. When Joan told me she was going to have our first child, I was so excited I could hardly speak. I felt the same excitement for each of our children. We decided to give our children Biblical names, you know, common names like John, Paul, and Mary. When our first boy was born, we named him Jeremiah John and called him Bo for short. Our second son we named Samuel Jason, but called him Bubba, because he was so big. Our little princess, Beka, was really Sarah Rebecca. When our Beka was born, Bo was four. They were all close enough in age to enjoy each other and give us lots of joy. My wife stayed home with them for those early years. Having three children ranging from seven to three is a real handful.

"On April 4, 1996, I was teaching my class as usual, when the door opened, and in walked the president of the school. He said in an uncanny tone of voice there was a gentleman in the hall who had to see me immediately. I opened the door and saw a highway patrolman standing there with that look that makes you know something is wrong. The patrolman asked if I was Steven

Lawrence Wilson. I said I was. He asked if my wife's name was Joan. I said, in a slumber type of voice, Joan is my wife's name. He said there had been an accident and asked if I would go to the hospital with him. I did not want to ask if anyone was hurt, for I already knew the answer.

"When I was seated, I asked him how serious the wreck was. He looked at me and said everyone in both cars was gone. I couldn't believe what he had just told me, so I said, 'You mean my wife and children were all killed?'

"I thought policemen were supposed to be strong like John Wayne, never showing any emotion. Well, he looked at me, and with tears coming down his face he said they were all killed in a head-on collision with a drunk driver. He said he had three children of his own and if he were to lose any one of them he would be heart broken. That was the most terrible moment in my life. But when I had to identify my family at the hospital, I could not control myself. I cried and cried.

"I wanted to die, but I knew there was a reason for what had happened. It took me a long time to get over losing my family. To get my mind stable again, I started working on my doctorate in Greek. In the spring of 1999 I received that doctorate degree. I decided I would put all my efforts into the work of the Lord.

"On April 1, 2000, I received a telephone call from Dr. Ben David Kent at Hebrew University in Jerusalem. Dr. Kent informed me there was only a handful of men in the world who had a doctorate in Greek and Hebrew. He said the university needed a Greek and Hebrew scholar to teach students with high I.Q.s. The university would pay me $52,000 a year, the expenses of an apartment or house, whichever one I wanted, plus a car. I had never been offered so much, just to teach. I knew the Lord had to be in it. It was He who made me work so hard to get a doctorate in Greek and Hebrew and allowed me the time and full concentration to obtain them. I decided the Lord must be leading me to Jerusalem.

"I had studied what the Bible says about the end times and I thought we were very near the end of the age. If I was wrong about the rapture, maybe the church would have to go through the tribulation and, if so, the Lord must be leading me to Jerusalem to protect me. I told Dr. Kent I would take the job. All I needed to know was when I should be there to start teaching. He said school would start on July 1, so that would give me three months to get packed and have all my affairs in order before I left.

"The three months went by so quickly I couldn't believe I was on a jet bound for Jerusalem. I wondered what it was going to be like to walk where Jesus walked and to see the things that most people only see on TV.

"The flight was over before I knew it, and I heard the voice of the stewardess say, 'Buckle your seat belts, we are about to arrive in Jerusalem.' When I stepped off the plane, I really thought I had made a mistake coming to Jerusalem. I looked around and everywhere there were soldiers with machine guns. It looked like Israel was at war. I walked through the terminal, and at the front door I looked around and saw a man with a sign that read, 'Dr. Wilson.' I walked over to him and said I was Dr. Steven Lawrence Wilson. He said he had a car and he would take me to my apartment. The apartment was nice, not large, but not small, just about the size I needed to be happy.

"I could not believe what I had just heard; I asked if it was true or just a rumor? I was told it was true, but until I saw Paul A. Messenger for myself, I would not believe he would be teaching here also. Dr. Messenger was the foremost Christian leader in the world. His headquarters were located in southern California, in a ten-story building. It was rumored he was giving everything up to come to Jerusalem to teach at the university. On July 1, the entire faculty met in the big conference room so we could meet each other. Dr. Kent introduced each member of the faculty and then said it was with great pleasure he would like to introduce Dr. Paul A. Messenger. I couldn't believe I would be teaching with a man of his stature. Dr. Messenger was the founder of 'The World Council of Religious Beliefs.' I met Dr. Messenger and told him how happy I was that he had decided to come to Hebrew University to teach.

"The next day, the students starting filling the chairs in the room. When the bell rang, I introduced myself and said this was my first year at the university. The students all seemed a little shy except for Michael D. Glispbe. I looked at the paper work the office had given me which stated he had an I.Q. that could not be rated.

"After the first day of classes, I went to the office and asked about Michael. I was told the test scores only go as high as 200 on the I.Q. scale, and they assumed his could be as high as 350. After I left the office I noticed Dr. Messenger was talking to Michael. They acted as if they were old friends.

"The next day I started to teach the structure of the Hebrew language. After class, Michael asked if he could talk to me about my method of teaching? He informed me he did speak Hebrew, but his grandmother never taught him how to read or write in Hebrew, but he wanted to learn all he could, even if it meant he had to work late at night to learn. I was impressed with his enthusiasm and asked, 'Could you come to my apartment some night and learn more?' He said he would enjoy doing that once a week.

"The first night Michael came over, I thought I could cover a lot of material, but things did not work out the way I had figured. Before I had a chance to begin teaching, he asked if I was a Christian, since I was from the United States. I told him I was a Christian; however, being from the U.S. did not make a person a Christian. When Michael asked a question, it seemed as if he already knew the answer to the question before I gave it them to him.

"Michael said he was very interested in Eschatology. He asked if I could give him some information on the end times. I said I would be delighted. I told him that sometime in the future there would be a man called the 'Antichrist,' who would come on the world scene and try to force everyone to take a mark or a number, 666. I told him the Antichrist would probably take scripture out of context and make it say what he wanted it to say. Michael asked if I could give him an example. I said I could give him one good example how the Antichrist might take a verse out of context.

"I stated, 'At the mid-point of the tribulation, the Antichrist will go into the temple and proclaim himself to be God. He may use Isaiah 14:13-14 to prove he is God, but he will have to take it completely out of context.' Michael was very eager to learn how one could take those verses out of context, so I showed him how it is done. In verses 13 and 14, one might say, 'I will ascend into the heavens, I will exalt my throne above the stars, I will sit also upon the mount of the congregation, I will ascend above the heights of the clouds, I am God.' I told him how people will take a little bit of a verse and not the whole verse, to make it say anything they want it to say.

"Michael seemed bewildered with the verses I gave, and I asked him if there was something wrong. He said, 'Those verses are verses that God should use all the time to prove he is God.' I showed him in verse 12 that the verse is talking about Lucifer. Michael became very dogmatic and said, 'It refers to God.'

"I decided it was best to stop the lesson at that point. Michael was increasingly agitated about the verses I used.

"The next day Dr. Messenger came by my office to ask how I was doing. I told him the day had gone well. He said he was a little concerned about something I had told a student, and maybe it would be best if I not get into Christian subjects. I asked who the student was, and he said it was Michael Glispbe. Dr. Messenger said that Michael was convinced that I took two or three verses out of context to prove my point. I informed him, 'I did not take anything out of context; I was showing him how people can take verses out of context to prove their point.'

"Dr. Messenger suggested it might be better if he took Michael under his wing and worked with him privately. I replied, 'That's a good idea; probably Michael can learn a lot more under the greatest Christian theologian of our time.'

"I thought about Michael that night and decided I would see what classes he was taking and what his major was. The next morning before classes began, I looked at his class schedule. I was amazed to see he was taking 27 hours and he did not have one major, but three. One major was Computer Programming, the second was Chemical Engineering, and the last major was Laser Technology.

"When a person is excited about his job and loves

what he is doing, it seems like time just flies by. That's the way it was with me that first year. The school year went by so quickly. Before I knew it, it was mid-April. School would be out May 1. There was a two-month vacation, and school would start back up on July 1. Dr. Messenger had taken Michael under his wing, and the two could be seen everywhere together. I talked to Michael from time to time but it always seemed he did not want to get into any deep discussions about anything. On April 30, I saw Michael and told him I would see him in July. He said this was the most productive year of his life. He indicated he was going to work with Dr. Messenger for the next two months, and if everything worked out he could be the richest man in the world within the next ten years.

"On May 3, I boarded a jet to go back home. During the flight I had a chance to think back about all the things I had done this past year. Working with Dr. Messenger and meeting Michael Glispbe were two of the high points. But probably the highest point of the whole year was being in Jerusalem. The places and things I saw would leave a lasting impression in my memory for the rest of my life.

"It was good to be back in a small town atmosphere. There weren't many things to do in Perry, but it really didn't make any difference, I was home. I decided I would go to Dallas for four or five days and see some of my old friends and professors.

"After visiting four or five of my friends, I went to the seminary to visit Dr. Charles H. Hale. Dr. Hale asked how I liked Hebrew University.

"I said, 'I really enjoyed teaching and sharing the knowledge I received from the seminary.' I mentioned the one student, Michael Glispbe, to Dr. Hale, how his I.Q. went off the scale. I also said there was something about him that was very unusual.

"Dr. Hale said, 'Unusual like what?'

"I told him I did not know — there was something that made me feel uncomfortable. After a lengthy conversation Dr. Hale asked if I would like to have supper with his family. I accepted without a hesitation. This would be the first home-cooked meal in almost a year.

"Dr. Hale was the only professor I could talk to on a first-name basis. He wasn't Dr. Charles Hale to me, he was Charlie. Charlie was about 15 years older than I was, but he acted more like a brother than a teacher. On the way to his house I had a chance to lean back and let my thoughts go back to college. The next thing I knew I was being shaken by Charlie, saying we were there. I apologized for falling asleep. 'The long trip over the last few days must be catching up with me.'

"There was another car pulling in behind us. Charlie said, 'That's my mother and father.'

"When I stepped out of the car, I noticed how young they looked, but realized they must be pretty old. I was wondering just how old Charlie's parents were, so I decided to ask him. He said his dad was almost 80 and his mother, 'Well, she is close to Dad's age.'

"While we were eating, I noticed it was getting a little dark outside. Charlie's wife Judy said, 'Looks like a big storm is moving in.'

"The rain started, and within seconds pea-size hail was coming down. The pea-size hail turned into golf-ball size, and the rain was coming down in buckets. Judy decided she had better turn on the TV to get the forecast, but the sirens went off before the weather man came on the screen. 'There must be a tornado on the radar.'

"As we headed for safety, I said, 'It's a comfort to

know if one were to die in a tornado or some other accident, he or she would be ushered into heaven immediately.'

"There was a dead silence when I made that statement. At first I thought the tornado was right on top of us; I was wrong. Tom said he and Debbie didn't believe in all that religious stuff.

"I never thought for a moment they weren't saved. With Charlie being a professor at a Christian University, I thought for sure his folks would be saved.

"The weather man said there was a hook on the radar, but it was gone now, so they canceled the tornado warning. Charlie invited me to stay over and we would go back to the seminary the next day to get my car so I could return to Perry. Lying in bed that night, I thought of how hard it would be to be a Christian most all your life and not have your parents saved.

"The next day I said good-bye to Charlie and said I would keep in touch with him from Jerusalem. He said next summer I must come back and visit and tell him all the exciting things that occurred that year. As I left the seminary, I felt a loneliness, similar to the kind of feeling I had when I lost my family.

"It took me about four hours to get back home to Perry, and upon my arrival I found a UPS package inside my door. The package was from Michael Glispbe. Inside the box were pictures of him and Dr. Messenger at the headquarters of the World Council of Religious Beliefs. Michael said how great it was to be in the United States and how free he felt. He said living in the Middle East with all the problems 'makes a person want to live somewhere else.' He said next summer he would like to come and visit me in Oklahoma, if it could be arranged.

"The two-month vacation was almost over. In one

week I had to be back in Jerusalem for the new school year. What a great summer I'd had, and if everything went the way I had figured, the next school year would fly by as quickly as the summer."

CHAPTER 3

I DECIDED I HAD been talking long enough, so I said, "We will resume our talk tomorrow." I asked if there were any questions before I returned to the New Jerusalem, that sits right above the earth. I could not believe my eyes, there must have been 200 hands raise in the air. I knew I could not answer all the questions, so I said, "I will answer as many questions as I can before I leave." The first question came from Mary Davenport. "Mary, what is your question?"

"When the rapture occurred, where were you, what were you doing, and was there a feeling or sensation when you were going up in the air?"

"On February 17, 2011, I was lecturing on the correct way to pronounce certain Hebrew words. At 10:07 the rapture occurred. That day is still as clear as if it occurred today. There were 22 students in my class, the students with high IQ's. I had barely begun teaching when a loud trumpet sounded, and in a twinkling of an eye I went through the ceiling and was going straight up, toward Jesus. I could not take my eyes off Christ. They were fixed on Him and Him alone.

"I had no feeling or sensation, like a person would have if they were falling. The only thing I did feel was a feeling that I was not alone. There were millions who had the same feeling of not being alone. I knew from what the Bible said that I had just received my incorruptible body. A body that could not sin, a body that was perfect.

It took only a second or two to be standing in the air with Christ and millions of other believers. The joy was unspeakable. I know, I had taught and believed the rapture would occur some day, but when it did occur, I was as surprised as every person who had just been raptured. We could not believe or comprehend what had just happened, but we knew where we were and what had happened.

"One thing I might say before we go to the next question is, the day before the rapture took place, we had a 20-minute discussion about the rapture in my Hebrew class. The 22 students in class were all Jewish. They were not believers in Christ. We were talking about certain words, and one student asked about the word Yeshua. I explained who Christ is and why I believed He was and is the promised Messiah. One student asked if I also believed in a disappearance of everyone called a Christian. I said, 'I do, and that disappearance is called the Rapture of the Church. One day in the very near future, all those who have placed their faith and trust in Jesus Christ will never die but be immediately raptured.'

"One student said, 'You mean you believe you are going to live forever without dying?'

" 'What I mean is, if the rapture occurs today, I will not die, but will disappear and go to be with Christ in heaven.'

"As I said earlier, the next morning at 10:07 I disappeared.

"Mary, does that answer your question?"

" Yes, thank you."

"James, what is your question?"

"Once you met the Lord in the air, did He take the Church directly to heaven, or did He take the Church some place else?"

"The first thing that happened when we met the Lord was that HE said, 'Welcome, my children.' We then went into heaven.

"The sight of heaven is unspeakable. There are no words that can describe what heaven is like, but I will try my best to describe what heaven is like. First I must say that heaven is different than some stories that have been told. When we met Christ, we were not in heaven. Heaven was a great distance away. The trip only took seconds. One moment we were traveling through what I would call a cloud, and the next moment we were seeing heaven. Once we arrived we had to go through a gate. Before the rapture, people would say Saint Peter was standing at the Pearly Gate, and if your name was written in the Book you could enter.

"In heaven there are 12 gates, but there is only one gate you can enter through. Well, when we arrived in heaven, everyone had to go through that gate in order to reach what is called the heavenlies. The 'heavenlies' is the place where God the Father is present. The Bible says that we must worship God the Father in spirit, because HE is spirit. With our corruptible body we could not look upon God the Father, but with our new incorruptible bodies, not only can we look upon Him, but we can also fellowship with Him.

"In the heavenlies there are three thrones. The middle throne is the place where God the Father is seated. Around the throne there are four living creatures called Cherubims. These creatures are there for one of two reasons. The first reason, they tell all of heaven about God. They say all day long, 'Holy, Holy, Holy, Lord God Almighty, who was, and is, and is to come.' The second reason is they represent the strength and power of God. God does not need anyone or anything to protect him.

The Cherubims are just a symbol of His strength and power.

"In the Bible it says there are streets of gold. When we think of gold, we probably think of the color, but pure gold is clear. Since the streets in heaven are made of pure gold, you can see through the streets.

"One thing I forgot to tell you about the gates is that they are pearls. The gates are giant pearls. Everyone must walk through the giant pearl, or the gate, in order to go into the heavenlies. The gates do not have doors because there is no need for doors in heaven. The gates stay open all the time because there is no night in heaven, only light. The darkness or the night is for those who are evil and corrupt. Also there is no need for the sun or the moon. The glory of God lights the heaven and the Lamb, or Christ, is our light.

"I said there were three thrones in heaven. There is a throne on each side of the middle throne which are symbolic of God the Son and God the Holy Spirit. I know it is very difficult to understand the trinity with human thinking, but when the thousand years are over and you receive your incorruptible bodies you will understand what I am saying. The only throne that is used is the middle throne. When we were judged by Christ at the Bema Seat, it was the middle throne Christ was seated on. Also, at the Great White Throne Judgement, the middle throne is the throne where Christ will sit. The three thrones represent the trinity. I know there will be more questions about heaven, so I will give you more information when the questions are asked.

"Bill what is your question?"

"What happened or where did you go after you left the heavenlies, and is heaven the same place as the heavenlies?"

"After we left the heavenlies, Christ took us through another gate that took us into heaven. It is very hard to explain the difference between the heavenlies and heaven. Like I said, 'One must have an incorruptible body and mind to comprehend or to understand the difference.' No one lives in the heavenlies except God the Father. Everyone else lives in heaven. In the heavenlies, we worship God as do the Cherubims and the angels. Everyone from Adam to Beverly Ann Shotley, the last person to become a Christian before the rapture occurred, lives in heaven. This is where Christ has prepared the mansions for the believers as stated in John 14:6. That will give you a small idea of heaven and the heavenlies.

"When we left the heavenlies, Christ took us through another gate into heaven. Once we went inside the gate, there were multitudes of people. I began to look around and coming toward me was my wife Joan, my two sons, Bo and Bubba, and my daughter Beka. I was so happy I was speechless. Bo, Bubba, and Beka were not children, but grown adults, 33 years old. You must remember in heaven there is no time or age or growing old or anything that would indicate time in heaven. By having a perfect mind you do not have to ask questions, the answer comes to your mind when you think, but remember, we created beings are not all knowing, only God is all knowing.

"Joan said she and the children would take me on a tour of heaven and I could meet anyone I wanted to meet. We began to walk, and as I looked around I was amazed at the beauty of heaven. No book or picture can really show or tell a person how beautiful and glorious heaven is. The first person I wanted to meet was the poor widow in Mark 12:41-44.

"Joan said, 'When we arrive at the area known as

the Gathering Place, you will meet Martha.'

"We continued to walk, and off in the distance I could hear multitudes of people talking. We walked toward the sound of voices and when we finally reached the area known as the Gathering Place, I could not believe my eyes. There were millions of people talking and singing and praising the LORD. The Gathering Place is the place where everyone goes once they leave the Heavenlies. There the new arrivals get to meet their loved ones that went before them and they also get to meet Old Testament saints and New Testament saints. The new arrivals also get to meet their guardian angels. I know many Christians did not believe in guardian angels, but once you are in heaven you will change your mind. I will tell you more about guardian angels in the days to come.

"At the Gathering Place I knew people whom I had never met before. I would look at them and know their name and know when they arrived in heaven. I was looking straight ahead when I sensed someone behind me. I turned and there was Martha. She looked at me and without her saying one word, I said, 'Martha.' She said she wanted to meet me and shake my hand. I was wanting to meet her, but she said she was wanting to meet me. I wondered, 'If we are supposed to have the answer before we ask the question, then why did I not know that Martha was wanting to meet me?'

"While I was thinking this, the LORD said to me, 'Even though you have the answer to your questions, there are some things that you will not know until it happens.' I told Martha, 'When I read in Mark about you giving all that you had, while others only gave some, I knew then that I wanted to meet you when I reached heaven.'

"After I met Martha, I asked Joan if Moses would be here also. Joan said, 'Moses will not be here today, but in a few days he will be here to meet all of the new arrivals.'

"I stated earlier that all new arrivals met at the Gathering Place. That was incorrect. All new arrivals met at the Gathering Place, except those of us who were raptured. Christ thought it was best for us to take a tour of heaven and sooner or later we would all get to the Gathering Place.

"Some people toured heaven for weeks before they reached the Gathering Place. Like I said, there is no time in heaven, but Christ does let us know about time if we think it. It may sound impossible, but I met every Old Testament saint in heaven and every New Testament saint that was there also.

"One thing I thought was strange was the first time I met the angels. I read about angels in the Bible, but to really meet one was quite an honor. In the Old Testament, we are introduced to Michael and Gabriel, the Arch Angels of God. The day I met them will always be a time I will never forget. To put it in plain English, angels are indescribable. In order to comprehend angels one must have an incorruptible body. At that time you will understand angels and see them the way they really are. Also you will be able to commune with God the Father, God the Son, and God the Holy Spirit.

"I will take two more questions then I must leave and go back to the New Jerusalem.

"Marty, what is your question?"

"You spoke about The Trinity, but what is The Trinity?"

I asked if everyone in the back could hear what I was saying? Those in the back said they could hear. I said, "This is so important I want to make sure everyone can hear.

"The Trinity has been explained in many, many ways.

One professor told me the Trinity is like an equilateral triangle. It has three equal sides; however, all three sides are independent of each other. Without all three sides, it is not a triangle. With all three sides you have one whole triangle. Another professor said, 'When I see an egg I always think of the Trinity. There is the shell, the yoke and the white. All three make up the whole egg, but without one you have nothing.' The human mind cannot understand the Trinity until it receives an incorruptible body. There are many illustrations a person could use, but we really cannot understand the Trinity through illustrations.

"Before the rapture I believed in the Trinity, but to understand it, I could not. If anyone tells you they understand the Trinity and can tell you whatever you need to know, they are liars. The easiest way to tell you of the Trinity is to say there is only one God, represented in three persons.

Once a person became a Christian, the Holy Spirit came to dwell within them. The Holy Spirit would guide and direct the Christian in his daily walk.

"Some people believed that a Christian could be demon possessed. If the Holy Spirit is present, the devil cannot be present. The Holy Spirit is working the same way as he did before. If you accept Christ as your personal Savior, the Holy Spirit comes to dwell within you. The Holy Spirit will let you understand as much as you need to understand about the Trinity.

"Remember, Faith is an integral part of Christianity.

"This will be the last question. Sandy, I know you have wanted to ask me something for the last two hours, so what is your question?"

"You mentioned earlier about the Bema Seat and the Great White Throne Judgements. Could you tell me more about those two events?"

"As I said earlier, we took a tour of heaven for 45 days, in earth time. Forty-five days after the rapture, the tribulation began. The very day the tribulation began, the Bema Seat Judgment also began in heaven."

"Brother Steven, can I interrupt?"

"Sandy, you know I never get mad if someone interrupts me to ask a question."

"Before you tell about the Bema Seat, you have stated twice there were 45 days after the rapture, before the tribulation began and 45 days after the rapture, before the Bema Seat began. Why were there 45 days before both of those two events, and did they occur at the same time?"

"The answer is yes, they did occur at the same time.

"In The Book of Daniel, chapter 12, verses 11 and 12 give us the total amount of days until the end of the tribulation and the setting up of the Thousand Year Reign of Christ on earth.

"The Thousand Year Reign of Christ is also called the Millennium. I have told you many times you are in the Thousand Year Reign of Christ. Daniel says, 'There are 1290 days until the end of the tribulation.' He also says, 'Blessed is he that waiteth for the 1335 days.' The difference is 45 days.

"When the Antichrist signed the peace treaty with Israel, one point that Israel wanted was for all the calendars to go back to the Old Testament's number of days, when there were 30 days in each month. Also in the Old Testament days at the end of every sixth year, Israel would add 30 days. The reason Israel did this is that they knew that each year would be short five days, so at the end of every sixth year they would add 30 days. By adding 30 days it would keep the seasons exactly where they should be. In chapter 11 of Revelation, verse 3, it says the two witnesses of God will prophesy 1260 days, which is 3-1/2 years, using the Old Testament calendar. Thirty days after the two witnesses prophesy, which is 1290 days, the Great Tribulation is ended.

"Before Christ sets up his reign on earth, He first judged the people on earth to see who would go into the Thousand Year Reign. This judgment was called 'The Judgment of the Nations.' Everyone was judged to see if he or she accepted Christ as their Savior. If they accepted, they could enter into the Millennium. If they took the number of the Antichrist, they were bound until the Great White Throne Judgment, which will occur after the 1000-year reign of Christ is over.

"There was a 45-day lull period after the tribulation, just as there was a 45-day lull period before the tribulation. There were many scholars and theologians who thought this would be the case, including Professor Hale. Many, many believers thought the tribulation would begin exactly when the rapture occurred. The Bible never taught or said anything about the tribulation beginning when the rapture occurred. The Bible did tell us what was going to happen, so people would know when the tribulation had begun. The Bible said sometime after the rapture the Antichrist would appear and sign a peace treaty with Israel for seven years. The signing of the peace treaty would start the tribulation.

"In order to get everything ready for the world to accept the Antichrist, there was a 45-day lull period. Oh yes, the answer to the second part of your question is about to be answered."

"Thank you, Brother Steven."

"Now I must finish the first question. When the tribulation began on earth, in heaven, the Bema Seat began for everyone from the first person to accept Christ on the Day of Pentecost to Beverly Ann Shotley, the last person to accept Christ before the rapture. One thing that has amazed me is that Christ knew who the first person would be to become a Christian on the Day of Pentecost, and He knew who the last person would be just before the rapture. Just imagine, the Church Age or the Age of Grace had to continue until Beverly became a Christian. The very year was numbered, the month, the week, the day, the hour, the minute and the second. The end of the age could not occur until that very second.

"At the Bema Seat, everyone, during the Church Age, appeared before Christ to answer what they had done after they became Christians. The Bema Seat is also called 'The Judgment Seat of Christ.' At the Bema Seat you could have received zero rewards or crowns, or as many as five rewards or crowns. If a person did nothing for the body or for Christ after he became a Christian, he received zero crowns or rewards. He was saved, but he or she was useless to the Body of Christ.

"On the other hand, I said there were five crowns or rewards. Each crown was named and each crown was given for a specific thing the Christian did in his or her life. The first crown was the incorruptible crown. This crown was given to those who could get mastery over the old man, or over sin. The second was the crown of rejoicing. This crown was given to those who were soul winners. The third crown was the crown of life. This crown was given to those who endured trials. Also it was given to those who were killed or martyred for their belief in Christ. The fourth was the crown of righteousness. This crown was given to those who loved His appearing and were looking forward to the rapture. The fifth was the crown of glory. This crown was given to those who were willing to feed the flock of God. This was also called the Pastor's Crown. At the Bema Seat, everyone did appear. Those things that were useless were burned up, like hay and stubble. Crowns were given for those things that were everlasting. We did not keep the crowns. We laid them at the feet of Christ. The crowns also represent the appointment or rulership on earth with Christ. Thus, I was given two crowns at the Bema Seat, and here on earth I have authority over two communities.

"The second question that was asked was about the Great White Throne Judgment. At the end of the Millennium, which is what you are in now, time will be over. Everyone who did not accept Christ as their Savior will appear at the Great White Throne. There will be no saved individuals there, only unsaved. They will be judged and cast into that place called Hell. There is no escape from the pit. It is a place of eternal torment and unbelievable anguish. There are degrees of Hell. If a person was in church every Sunday and he heard and knew what the gospel said and he still rejected Christ, he would be cast into the worst part of Hell. On the other hand, if a person in the jungle had never heard of Christ, he would be cast into the lesser part of Hell. Any way you look at it, it is not a place where one would want to go. But because of the sinful nature of man, he goes there of his own free will. Hell was not made for man, but for the Devil and his angels.

"That should answer your question about the Bema Seat and the Great White Throne Judgment. There is one more thing before I leave. I said the Bema Seat started at the same time the tribulation began. The Bema Seat lasted for 3-1/2 years earth time. After the Bema Seat, the Marriage Supper of the Lamb began. The Marriage Supper was the time that Christ presented His

Bride, The Church, to heaven. His Bride was presented to heaven spotless and without blemish. The Marriage Supper lasted the same amount of time as did the Bema Seat, 3-1/2 years. But it took place during the last half of the tribulation. During the Marriage Supper, the Old Testament saints served the Bride. The Old Testament saints took a lot of pride in serving the Bride, and the Bride felt honored to have the Old Testament saints serving them.

"We have spent a lot of time this day talking about the things that occurred just before the rapture and what happened in heaven during the tribulation period on earth. Tomorrow we will resume our talks, and you might be prepared with more interesting questions." With that, I disappeared and went back to the New Jerusalem.

CHAPTER 4

"**YESTERDAY**, we covered some questions you had from my opening talk. Today, I want to continue where I left off with my life story, and if there is time, I will entertain more questions later.

"My two-month vacation was almost over, and I started packing for my trip back to Jerusalem. My second year of teaching would be starting on July 1. I was looking forward to the new school year. The new students, new teachers and working with Dr. Messenger would be an experience beyond words.

"The fall of 2000 and the spring of 2001 was such a thrill, I wished school could be year round, but I supposed everyone would get burned out sooner or later. I was thinking I might have a chance to share the Gospel with Michael this year and lead him to Christ. I could only wait and see what would happen when school started.

"On June 28th I flew back to Jerusalem so I could have everything ready in my apartment and at school before the students came back. On July 2, 2001, the students were swarming the halls looking for their classes and seeing if the teachers were in the same rooms or if they had been moved to other rooms.

"I was sitting at my desk when Michael Glispbe walked in and said hello. I asked Michael what courses he was taking this year. He stated he was not sure at this point; Dr. Messenger was going to direct him in the right direction. He said he would get back with me before the day was over; there was so much he wanted to talk about.

"My new first-hour class started right on time. I thought there would be one student who impressed me with his knowledge or his wit, but I was mistaken. The new group were just average-smart kids. My third-hour class was the class I was looking forward to teaching. Michael was supposed to be in that class, and he was so intelligent it was mind-boggling. I remember what Michael had said last year about being the richest man in the world one of these days. I don't know how he thinks that will be accomplished; he is not a rich kid.

"When my third hour class began, most of the students were the same ones from last year. I decided I would let everyone tell what they had done over their two-month vacation. The first student took three minutes to tell the class what he had done during his vacation.

"It was boring!

"Student after student told the class what they had accomplished. I wondered to myself, if these really were high IQ students, they were not communicating their thoughts very well. The last to speak was Michael.

"Michael began by telling the class how he and Dr. Messenger spent the two months at the headquarters of the World Council of Religious Beliefs' building. He told how the headquarters building was divided into different groups. Each group was a different belief, or one might say a different religion.

"Michael said, 'It is Dr. Messenger's idea if we can get all the religions to accept or believe one thing, we can then bring all religions under one banner.' I have so much respect for Dr. Messenger and everything he stands for I could not believe what Michael had just told the class. Michael was saying that Dr. Messenger was trying to get all religions to believe one thing. If it was a belief in Christianity that's fine, but what if it was a mixture of all religions. At Dallas Theological Seminary we called this hodge-podge, 'The Ecumenical Movement.' Could Dr. Messenger really be involved in a movement that would put all the religions together?

"Michael continued to talk and tell how different leaders of major religions would come to the headquarters and meet with Dr. Messenger. They would spend hours putting together plans how one day, in the near future, all people would belong to one church. Michael stated if everyone belonged to one church and everyone believed one thing, the world would be a much safer place to live. Within one month, Michael said Dr. Messenger introduced him to the leaders of 22 religions. Michael did not know why Dr. Messenger always would introduce him, but he assumed Dr. Messenger was being kind because Michael was his guest for the summer.

"One statement that Michael made almost caused me to fall out of my seat. One person Dr. Messenger introduced to Michael was Dr. Mohammed, the founder of a new religion based in Babylon. The new religion is called 'The Fellowship of Believers.' Under this new religion, all persons are considered equal. Women are equal to men, children are equal to adults. No one is discriminated against or held in higher esteem than anyone else. Michael noticed that Dr. Messenger and Dr. Mohammed stood and whispered back and forth for a couple of minutes before he was introduced. When he finally met Dr. Mohammed, instead of shaking hands, Dr. Mohammed bowed and kissed Michael's right hand. Michael was surprised but thought it was a custom from Iraq.

"Dr. Messenger told Michael, 'One of these days Babylon will be the center of all religions.' Dr. Messenger also told Michael, 'I am seriously considering moving my headquarters to Babylon, so I can be closer to the new religion.' As I sat and listened to the things Michael was saying, my mind went to the Book of The Revelation. Revelation states in the Tribulation there will be a one world religion located in Babylon. It will be a false religion that will lead people astray. The leader of that false religion will be the False Prophet. I started to wonder, 'Could Dr. Mohammed be the False Prophet, or could Dr. Messenger be the False Prophet?' I knew nothing of Dr. Mohammed, but I knew a lot of Dr. Messenger. Dr. Messenger was known all over the world for being such a loving man and a person who cared about all people. It had been said that he was one of the ten richest men in the world. He was always giving millions of dollars away to the needy and to different charities. If Dr. Messenger was the False Prophet, he did not fit the pattern I would have expected.

"The class was spellbound by the things Michael was telling. It seemed as if he had made everything up before he came to class. I wondered to myself if Michael had made all these things up or had they really happened. Michael continued to tell the class about his two-month vacation. He said when he was in the Simi Valley area he met a professor friend of Dr. Messenger who showed him many tricks in writing computer programs.

"Michael said Dr. Messenger was going to form a company that would put all computer companies out of business within 12 years. Dr. Messenger told Michael that he, Michael, would be the CEO of the new company. Michael did not say how all the computer companies in the world would be put out of business, but it was a sure thing.

"Michael also told about a new weapon that he

worked on for four days. He said it was such a secret there were only three people in the world who knew anything about it. As Michael continued to tell about his vacation, I looked around the room and all the students seemed to be in a trance. They were drinking in everything Michael was saying. I have to admit, while I sat there listening I caught myself almost in a trance. I think if Michael would have asked if there was anyone wanting to jump off a bridge at that time, everyone in the room would have jumped.

"The way Michael stood, the way he held his head, the way he moved, his confidence in himself and what he was saying reminded me of the great politicians of the world. If he could hold a crowd's attention the way he was holding this class' attention, he could sway the entire world into believing anything he might say or do.

"I told Michael there were only 15 minutes left, and if he could finish that would be fine, but if it was going to take more than 15 minutes he could finish the next day. Michael said there was only one thing remaining that he would like to share with the class. He said he had a dream that was so real it seemed as if he was present in the dream.

"In the dream, a man came toward him, bowed and said, 'The future belongs to you, Michael. I will show you what will happen in the immediate future.'

"Michael said he saw two animals in his dream; one was a bull and the other was a bear. The bear was big, strong, agile and cunning. She was alone for a very long time, but soon there were two bears, then three, four, five; there were so many he could not count how many bears there were. The bull was very different. He stood alone. He did not fight with the bears, but he overcame them with his wit and with rumors. He told the man that he did not understand the dream. The man said he would tell Michael what the dream means.

"He said, 'Michael, my son, the bear is the New York Stock Exchange. It is the biggest and strongest stock exchange in the world. It has made millions for some men, and it has taken everything from others. The New York Stock Exchange stood alone for many, many years. Then another stock exchange opened, and another, and another, until there were so many they could not be numbered.' The man told Michael that he was the bull. He told Michael that he would set up a brand new stock exchange that would put all the others out of business. He told Michael the name of the new stock exchange would be the 'Global Stock Exchange.' The Global Stock Exchange would control all the stock in the world. He also told Michael that he would be the richest man in the world and would be in control of the entire world within 15 years.

"When Michael finished, no one said a word; they were speechless. If everything Michael said was true, who could Michael be?

"Could he be the coming Antichrist?

"Could he be someone who goes off the deep end every now and then?

"Could he be like one of those writers who always has a good story to write about and is seeing what the reaction is of his audience?

"There was not much time left, so I let the students leave early. I told Michael the things he shared with us were very fascinating. I asked if he would like to share anything the next day. He said there was something he would like to say, but everyone might think was losing his mind. I told him to think about it that night, and if he would like to tell the class the next day, he could use 20 minutes to do so.

"That night I thought about what was said by Michael and the time span that was in his dream. Within 15 years he would be the richest man in the world. That would mean by 2016 Michael would be richer than anyone else. I opened my Bible and began to read what Daniel had said about the end times and what Revelation said about the False Prophet and the Antichrist. The more I read, the more uneasy I became. Was I right in the middle of everything that was about to happen in the last days? What I thought about earlier in class about Dr. Messenger being the False Prophet and Michael being the Antichrist, could it be true?

"All of a sudden it hit me like a bolt of lightning. I thought back to last year when I first went into the classroom. I was the new teacher, and the students knew it was my first year here. I remember very clearly what happened that night. I asked the students if they would like to tell the class what they had done on their vacations before class began. I asked each student to tell us what they had done. When I asked Barry Cohen, he said what he was about to share with the class was very, very confidential, and if anyone told others what he was about to say, he could get into a lot of trouble. Barry said his uncle was one of the leading archaeologists in Israel and what his uncle had found would astound the world if it were revealed. Barry asked for everyone to come into a tight circle and he would tell us what had been found. Once everyone was in the circle, in a very low-toned voice he stated that his uncle had found the Ark.

"He said, 'If it is revealed that the Ark has been found, it could start another war with the Arabs.' I could not control my excitement. The Bible said that Israel would start the animal sacrifices during the Tribulation. I also believed the Ark would be found and placed in the Tribulation

Temple. If this was true, the Tribulation could not be that far off. I was so excited I asked Barry if he could tell us where the Ark was located?

"He said it was at his uncle's house in the basement. After class I asked Barry if I could go to his uncle's house and see the Ark. Barry whispered, 'The only time you can come to my uncle's house is tonight. A couple of the other students will be by at seven to pick you up.' At seven I was waiting outside, and right on time Barry's friends showed up.

"His uncle's house was 10 minutes away. Upon entering the house something seemed strange. The house was not what I expected for an elderly man. We went to the basement, and inside one room was where the Ark was supposed to be. Before we went in, Barry told us that the Ark puts off so much electricity that it could kill me or anyone who touched it. Barry opened the door and turned on the light, and in the middle of the floor was a wooden container. 'The Ark is in the container,' Barry said, 'And if you want to see the Ark, you will have to open the top of the container.' I walked over to the container and lifted the lid. Out jumped Michael and Kevin. They scared me so badly I thought I would have a heart attack. I must admit, I did wet my pants from the fright. They all got quite a laugh out of my gullibility.

"I figured Michael told all those stories in order to set me up again like he did last year, telling me about the dream and meeting a large number of important people. He must think I had forgotten about last year. Well, I almost had, but he would have to get up really early in the morning to outwit me again. This time it was going to be a joke on him. I would go ahead and play his game, but this time I would know what he was trying to do. I would just wait for an opportunity to let the joke backfire.

"The next day in class I asked Michael if he wanted to add to his story about his vacation. He said he would like to add one thing. He stated, 'While I was in California I met a man by the name of Tim Cabot. Tim had an idea that was so great it would make people think about getting one of these if the price was right. The idea that Tim had was a fully functional robot that looks like a man, talks like a man, walks like a man, has artificial blood that looks real, and can reason to a certain extent. The plans have been drawn up for over a year, but the cost is so high Tim does not have the money to begin building the robot. Tim says everything is ready except for the money and one other thing. The one thing that is needed is something that looks like real skin. Tim has tried many things, but nothing has worked yet.'

" 'Dr. Messenger said it would probably take someone with a degree in Chemical Engineering to discover a substance that would look like skin, feel like skin, and breath like skin. I am so intrigued by the thought of a robot that would look exactly like me, I am going to devote all my spare time to developing something similar to skin. And, Dr. Messenger told me he will pay all the expenses if I can develop a synthetic skin.'

"I asked Michael if there was anything else, and he said, 'No, that's it.' I began to teach the class from my plans.

"The first couple of weeks went just the way I had planned. I did not see Michael very much, only in class. I was told he was working very hard to develop synthetic skin. The third week things turned completely around. After class one day Michael asked if he could drop by after school and talk. I said that would be fine.

"After school, Michael stopped by and we had a friendly chat. He said he had been spending all his extra time the last two weeks trying to develop synthetic skin, but it was useless and could not be done. 'There is no way synthetic skin can breathe like real skin.'

" 'Michael, the best way to approach the problem is with a brand new outlook on things. Take a couple of weeks off and then look at it from another view point. The way I try to solve a problem is to take the obvious and reverse it.'

"Michael asked if it would be okay if he spent most of his free time the next two weeks with me? That was exactly what I wanted. The time that we would spend together the next two weeks might be the only opportunity that year I would have to share Christ with him. I told Michael it would be great to spend some time together.

"After class the next day, I told Michael I would cook supper if he would like to come by my apartment around six-thirty. Michael was at my apartment right on time. After supper we sat and talked for a while, and then Michael started asking questions like he had last year.

"Michael asked me, 'Why can't I understand the Bible when I read it? When you read the Bible, you know what it is saying. I have read a lot about the end times but don't understand a word it says. Could you help me understand what the Bible is saying?'

"I told Michael, 'The Bible says one must be Born Again in order to understand the Word of God. One must accept Jesus Christ as his personal savior in order to be Born Again. One day, everyone will bow before Christ and acknowledge that he is God. You can do it now while you have a chance, or you can put it off until some other time. We are not guaranteed one more minute on earth; however, we could die this day. So it is best not to put things off; you may never have another opportunity. If a person dies without accepting Christ as their savior, they will have to appear at the Great White Throne and then be cast into Hell.' I then asked Michael if he would like to accept Christ as his savior. He said because of his Jewish belief he could not do that, but if he changed his mind he would let me know.

"Michael asked, 'What about a thing called the Tribulation? When will it start and what will happen during that time? It is about seven years in length, right?'

"I answered, 'Yes.'

"I said, 'There will be a man who will come on the world scene that the Bible calls the Antichrist. He will deceive people into believing he is a man of peace. He will become the President of the revised Old Roman Empire. The European Common Market is the revised Roman Empire. When the rapture occurs, this man will come on the world scene. Forty-five days after the rapture, The Antichrist will sign a seven-year peace treaty with Israel. He will guarantee the peace of Israel, and he will state that an attack on Israel is the same as an attack on the Common Market. Mid-way through the tribulation, the Antichrist will go into the Temple of God and proclaim himself to be God.'

"Michael asked me a question which caught me off guard. He asked, 'Is the Antichrist a real man or is he an alien?'

"I said, 'Michael, the Antichrist is a real man. He is a liar, a murderer, a thief and a deceiver. The Bible says at the mid-point of the tribulation there is war in heaven. The devil is kicked out of heaven and cast down to earth. At that time, he will indwell the Antichrist.'

"Michael did not say anything, he just sat and stared out the window.

"Michael asked me another question that I found very hard to answer. 'If the Antichrist rules the world, how does he take over all the wealth that the world has?'

"I said I did not know how the Antichrist could do that, but if we looked at some of the things he would have to take over, maybe we could see how it might be done. 'One area he must take over is the buying power of all the people in the industrialized world. One thing he could do would be to set up a new credit card company. Let's say, if he charged 8 percent interest for everything under $10,000 and 7 percent interest for everything over $10,000, he could put all the other credit card companies out of business. In chapter 13 of the Book of The Revelation, it says the Antichrist will have control over everyone, and without his mark or number no one can buy or sell or even have a job. So, he must have control of the economy of the entire world.'

"The more we talked, the more Michael wrote. At one point I thought he was writing everything I said, but when I questioned him, he said he was mainly writing down his own thoughts.

"Michael asked what other areas I thought would have to be controlled in order to have world domination? I told Michael there were three other areas that would have to be controlled in order to control the whole world. 'First is computers. If someone controlled all the computers in the world, he would control the world of finances. Second is stocks and bonds. If one person had control of all the stock markets in the world or if he had the only stock market in the world, he could bring the world to its knees. Third is currency. If someone was in control of the only currency in the world, he would have control of every person in the world. To sum it all up, the total control of the world lies in four things: credit cards, stocks and bonds, currency, and last, but the most important, is computers. Without the computer the other three are useless.'

"While Michael wrote, I could see a real change in him. His eyes started to glimmer, and he would smile and then laugh.

"After a while I asked, 'What's so funny?'

"He looked at me and said, 'Everything is at my fingertips, if I can just put the puzzle together.' I did not know or understand what he was talking about, so I watched him write. After 20 minutes he said he was finished. He asked if he could come back the next night and learn more from the Bible? I told him it was great he was taking an interest in the Word of God. He looked straight into my eyes and said, 'You don't really know how interested I am in the Bible. If you did, you would be amazed.'

"The next day Michael said he would have to cancel our study that night. He said he and Dr. Messenger had an emergency trip to take to California that could not wait.

"When they came back from California, Michael was totally different. It seemed he had changed overnight. His personality became rude toward everyone, except me. I could still talk to him, but he was short and to the point. He told me he was devoting all his spare time to the things that would make him rich. I thought Michael and Dr. Messenger must be into something very important, since they were always together, going over notes, writing things down, and rushing off.

"One week before Thanksgiving in the United States, I received a long distance telephone call from Dr. Hale in Dallas. He told me of a new company by the name of ICAN. He said, 'It is a new credit card company that is being tested in Texas, New York and California. I predict it will spread all over the world because of the low interest rates. The interest rate is a fixed 8 percent for everything below $10,000. If your balance is over $10,000, the interest rate drops to 7 percent.'

"I asked if he had received one of the new cards and he said, 'Yes, I have.' He also said if the card becomes usable all over America, he will destroy all the other cards he has. He said, 'The best thing about the card is if you transfer your balance from other cards to the new ICAN card, the fixed interest rate is 5 percent until the balance is paid off. He said this new card will rethink interest rates in America and all over the world.'

"That night I was thinking about the things Michael and I had talked about. How did my idea become reality, or was it just coincidence?

"The more I thought, the more I decided it was not coincidence. I turned on my computer and logged into the Internet. I typed in the word ICAN. The program began to play a tune, and on the scene was the introduction. I watched as it continued to give the public all the information one would need to receive the new card. The commercial informed the viewer that they 'deserved to have the things they wanted or needed. The high interest rates that other companies are charging keep you from buying and fulfilling your dreams. The low interest rates from our company make it possible for YOU to get what YOU deserve. The high interest rates that other credit card companies charge make you say I CAN'T buy anything, but with the low interest rates we charge, you will be able to say ICAN buy what I DESERVE. Don't be the last person to get the card, apply now and it will be rushed to you so you can begin getting the things you deserve.'

"The commercial made it hard not to order the card. At the end of the commercial it gave the name of the company. The name of the new company was 'International Credit Association of Nations,' shortened to ICAN. The headquarters was located in southern California. Dr.

Messenger's headquarters were also located in southern California. I decided I would check with some of my friends in America the next day after class and see what they could tell me of the new company.

"After all my classes, I went straight home and called an investor friend of my mind in New York City. We talked for a while, and then I said, 'Dan, could you give me any information on a new company by the name of ICAN?'

"He said, 'I have already checked on the company and have bought stock in it. It is moving so fast if you are wanting to get on the band wagon, now is the time to do so. The company has been in business for about 30 days, but it is making money like crazy.'

"I asked, 'Who are the backers or who is putting up all the money?'

"He stated, 'I don't know, but I have heard the person backing the new company is one of the richest men in the world.'

"I also asked if any of the officers were named, and he said the only person named was the CEO. If that is the only officer named, I guess that was a beginning, so I asked who the CEO was?

"He said, 'I have never heard of this person, and it is impossible to find out anything about him. All records of this man are being kept secret. The man's name is Diabolos. Undoubtedly the people that set up this new company are not wanting to be named.' I thought to myself, 'The Greek meaning of the word Diabolos is the Devil.'

"The next day after class I asked Michael if he would wait, I needed to ask him a question. He waited, impatiently. I asked, 'Are you getting enough sleep and are you eating right?' I did not want to sound like his mother, but he did not look well.

"He said, 'My health does not matter. There are more important things than eating and sleeping. I have but a short time to accomplish everything that has to be done.' He turned and started to walk out the door, and that is when the idea hit me like a Mack truck.

"When he opened the door to walk out, I said, 'Diabolos.'

"He stopped and turned, and with a look that could have killed, he said with a harsh tone in his voice, 'No one ever calls me Diabolos. I hate that name, and I hate my parents for giving me that name.' He walked over to me, and with his nose next to mine he said, 'Don't ever call me that again.' He turned and walked out of the classroom.

"My suspicions were correct. He was the CEO of the new company. The things we had talked about and the notes he took were now becoming fact. I now knew who Michael really was, but there was nothing I could do to change what was about to happen. The only thing I could do was not to share anything else with him, but I had shared so much already. I had told him almost everything that would occur in the tribulation and what would precede the rapture. Michael knew what was needed and the different areas he would have to concentrate on in order to control the world. I could not believe what I had done.

CHAPTER 5

"**THE NEXT DAY** before classes started, Michael walked into my room and said he was sorry for what he had said the day before. 'I have only been sleeping for two or three hours a day, and I am so tired I am saying things without thinking.'

"I told him that I did not take any offense to what he said and everything was forgiven.

"The first semester was almost over, and the students and teachers would have a two-week vacation before we had to be back for the second semester. I decided I had been in Jerusalem long enough, so I made plans to fly back to Oklahoma. A rest was what I needed.

"Two days before the semester was over, Michael came into my room excited and beaming from ear to ear. I asked, 'What has you so excited?'

"He exclaimed, 'I have just finished writing and de-bugging my master computer program!'

" 'I did not know you were writing a program.'

"He said, 'Remember back in August when we talked about what a person would have to do to have control of the economy of the world? You said computers were the real answer. I have written a program that is so sophisticated, but user friendly, it will replace all computer operating systems. I have de-bugged the program and put information into it to see what the result will be, and it works perfectly.' Michael decided he would take as much time as needed to ascertain the creditability of his new program before he would attempt to sell it.

"I told Michael I was off to Oklahoma for two weeks, and when I returned I would see how his new program was going.

"Being home in Oklahoma was great. I could relax and not have any worries about what had happen in the last six months. I called Dr. Charlie Hale and told him I was on a two-week vacation and asked if I could visit him one day next week. He said the school would be closed for two days because of an International Conference Meeting in Washington, D.C. I spent most of the remainder of that week visiting friends and seeing relatives. Monday morning I awoke early and drove to Dallas to meet Charlie. We had lunch, and then I told him the reason I wanted to talk. I told him about Michael and that I thought he would be the coming Antichrist.

"Charlie said, 'I don't believe that we Christians will know who the Antichrist is before the rapture. If we did, we could alter events, and maybe some fanatic might even try to assassinate him. He could be like an Anti-Christ.'

"I told him about the idea I had for the credit card company and within three months it was reality. I also told Charlie about Michael's middle name being Diabolos. Charlie looked at me and said, 'You know in the Greek Diabolos means the Devil.'

" 'I know,' I commented, 'that's what scares me.' I also told Charlie about the new program that Michael says will replace all operating systems in the world. 'If that is true, he could control all the world's computers.'

"Charlie said, 'I thought the Antichrist would come out of the Common Market, not Jerusalem. I really don't think you should worry about Michael; probably nothing will come from his or your ideas.'

"I drove back to Oklahoma feeling a lot better. I guess I was really blowing things out of proportion. I thought back how TV preachers made some really big predictions that never came true. I know the TV audience would believe what they would say, and when it did not happen they made excuses to cover up their ignorance of the Word of God.

"I spent the rest of the week doing nothing. On Saturday I flew back to Jerusalem and decided to look at Michael in a new light. I could not assume he was someone that I thought he was or that I might want him to be. He was just a 19-year-old boy excited about college. Also, I believed he was probably spell-bound by Dr. Messenger, but who wouldn't have been?

"Monday started the new semester. I had a different outlook, and when I saw Michael I asked how he was doing and how his program was going. He said he found one or two bugs, but other than that, everything was great. I noticed Michael was wearing some new clothes and asked if his parents sent them to him. He said he had a job and he was using that money to buy the things that he needed. Within the next three weeks, Michael was driving a new BMW, wearing a new Rolex watch, wearing custom-made clothes and sporting rings that would choke a cow. I was not going to be negative. I thought his new job must pay really well but, I must admit, I figured the money came from his credit card company. The weeks went by so fast it did not seem possible 2002 was only a few days away.

"The new year started out cold and snowy. Everyone said they couldn't remember it being so cold. January 5th would be remembered in Jerusalem for years to come. It was so cold that people were using make-shift, pot-belly heaters to keep warm. In one Jewish school the electricity went out, so one of the teachers asked if it would be okay to use one of the pot-belly heaters. She was given permission, and within one hour the room was warm and comfortable. Before anyone knew what was happening, the heater had used up all the oxygen in the room. The teacher and the students had passed out. One student tried to get to the door, but she fell and knocked the heater over. The wood inside the heater started a fire, and within minutes the school was totally engulfed in flames. The school had a total of 963 students. Fire trucks began arriving, as did the police, and ambulance after ambulance. Firemen were risking their own lives to save the children inside.

"One hour after the fire started the news medias were asking for anyone in the Jerusalem area to go to the nearest hospital to give blood. There was also a request for help in the hospitals, if anyone was willing to donate their time.

"Dr. Kent said, 'If anyone wants to help, they should leave immediately and go to the hospitals.' Some students went and others decided they might be in the way. I was on my way out the door when Michael asked if I was going to the hospital.

"I said, 'I think they could use all the help they can get, and that's where I'm headed.'

"He asked if he could ride with me, and I said, 'Sure, but we need to leave now.'

"They were bringing children in cars, trucks, and any way they could get them to the hospitals. This hospital was in total chaos. In each hospital there were morgues being set up for those who had already died. I heard one doctor say in a whisper, 'More than 700 of the children are feared dead. It may take days to identify the dead. Some of the bodies were burned beyond recognition.'

"The hospital asked if I could work in the burn unit. Michael also asked if he could help in the burn area, and they sent both of us there. There were too many victims and not enough helpers. We had to dress in totally sterile uniforms and wear a mask. I did everything they told us to do in the five-minute crash course they gave us. I was too busy to see what Michael was doing, but when I looked up, I noticed he had tears in his eyes.

"I asked, 'How do you feel? Are you going to be okay?'

"He said he would overcome his grief. He said, 'The kids that live will be scarred for life. With the technology we have, why can't someone invent some type of skin that will go over burn victims, so there will not be any scars?' There was nothing I could say; Michael was right.

"Being in the hospital all day was exhausting, but what bothered me more was to stand there and watch small children die and not be able to do anything. I looked around for Michael, but one of the nurses said he had gone. I figured he had seen enough. For a 19-year-old, he had seen more in one day than most people see in a lifetime. I informed one of the doctors I would stay up all night with the children if they had a place where I could rest for a couple of hours.

"At four in the morning one of the doctors came in and asked if I could help out for at least another 12 hours. I said I could help as long as they needed me. I asked the doctor if anyone had come up with a count of the number of dead persons. He said he had called all the hospitals, and the numbers he had been able to put together were 137 still alive. He said it was the worst fire in the history of Jerusalem.

"At ten, there was a telephone call for Dr. Myers in the burn unit. I thought it was another hospital calling to give more information on the dead. As Dr. Myers talked to the person on the other end, his appearance changed. He was getting excited, and he asked the person on the other end of the line in a loud voice if he could come to the hospital immediately, and then he hung up the receiver.

"Dr. Myers asked for all the nurses and helpers to step outside for a short statement. Outside in the corridor, he stated, 'I have just talked to a young man who was helping in the burn unit. The young man was grieved about the scars the children will have from the burns. He went back to the university and started to work on an idea he had. Overnight, he says he has developed a solution that will work on burn victims. The young man is on his way to the hospital right now.'

"Within 20 minutes Michael appeared in the burn unit. Dr. Myers talked with Michael, and then he went outside and talked with the parents of one of the children they did not think would live. Dr. Myers came back in and requested that the young girl be prepared for surgery. The operation lasted only 20 minutes. When Dr. Myers came back into the room, he was smiling. He asked for everyone to listen to what he was going to say.

" 'The operation went well, but the next two hours will tell if it is a success.' Michael was standing next to Dr. Myers while he was telling about the operation. Dr. Myers continued, 'If the operation is a success, it is because of the invention of a solution that works with real skin to rejuvenate the cells. Michael Glispbe went back to the university and worked all night to invent this solution. Let's all pray it will be a success.'

"One hour came and went, and then the second hour passed. Dr. Myers decided after two hours and 20 minutes he would check to see if anything had happened.

When he lifted the gauze that had the special solution in it off the arm, he could not believe what he saw. The area where the burn had been was completely healed.

"At that time Dr. Myers started shouting out orders and making telephone calls to all the hospitals in the Jerusalem area where burn victims had been taken. I heard him say to someone on the other end of the telephone, 'I don't care what people think or what they will say, the method works! We can save hundreds of lives!'

"Michael came into the burn unit smiling and crying at the same time.

"I said, 'I'm tired and ready for a break.' We went outside in the fresh air and just sat in the cold. He explained how he had invented the artificial skin. What he told me I could not believe. It was beyond my wildest dreams.

"Michael said after he left the hospital he began to walk and think. He thought of different chemicals he could put together, and it dawned on him what would work. He called Dr. Messenger and told him what his idea was and asked if Dr. Messenger would meet him at the university. At the university, Dr. Messenger agreed to help with the experiment. Michael gave Dr. Messenger a shot to put him to sleep. After Dr. Messenger was asleep, Michael then turned on a burner and burned Dr. Messenger's arm. He awoke three hours later and asked if the graft worked. Michael said, 'We will soon find out,' and removed the gauze. The burned area on Dr. Messenger's arm was completely healed. Michael asked Dr. Messenger if there was any pain in his arm, and Dr. Messenger said his arm felt fine. Michael said the solution should work with any skin. He said once a person is burned, you must remove the dead skin. You then apply the special solution to the area where the skin was removed, and then you apply the artificial skin. You then place a piece of gauze, which has been soaking in the special solution, on the artificial skin. Within two hours, the artificial skin will graft to the burned area. The special solution and the artificial skin make the burn area heal within hours. The special solution also stops infection. The real test will be in the next 24 hours. If the body does not reject the make-believe skin, then it is a success.

"Within 24 hours, Dr. Messenger's arm did not show any sign of rejecting the artificial skin. Michael called the hospital and asked about the young girl, whom they had not expected to live. Dr. Myers said, 'She is doing fine as far as the burns are concerned. They have operated on her every 30 minutes until all the burned skin was removed and replaced with the artificial skin. There is no infection and her body is not rejecting the skin. She may still die, but it won't be from the burns. She inhaled a lot of smoke, and at this time her lungs are still trying to shut down.'

"Michael questioned Dr. Myers, 'Since it works on burned skin, maybe it would work on lungs.'

"Dr. Myers said, 'We will try the treatment on one lung. If it works, she will probably live.' Two days later, Michael said he had talked to Dr. Myers, and the lungs had healed just like the rest of her body had healed.

"Michael said Dr. Messenger is helping him with the patent rights for the special solution and for the substitute skin. He said hospitals all over the world are calling and requesting both for their burn victims. The invention will make Michael into a millionaire overnight.

"I thought back to the beginning of the school year when Michael was telling about his vacation and how he had met a man in California. The man's name was Tim Cabot, and he had an idea about a robot. Michael said he spent two weeks trying to invent synthetic skin but nothing ever worked. Well, if what Michael said about his vacation is true, he now has synthetic skin or artificial skin.

"I did not have a chance to talk with Michael for the next three weeks. On his way out of class one day he said the news media wanted interviews and statements about the solution and artificial skin he had invented. He requested of me, 'Please do not say anything about the substitute skin. If the news media finds out the substitute skin is that of a slain lamb, they might charge me for cruelty to animals. I have received my patent, and there is talk I am in line for the Nobel Prize.'

"I asked, 'Have you received any money from this invention?'

" 'I have received over six million dollars.' In three weeks he had received over six millions dollars; that is two million a week. In one year he would make over one hundred million dollars; I was speechless.

"I wondered to myself if he was receiving any money from the credit card company. I had heard over the news that the card would be distributed nationwide in the U.S. in three months.

"The next time I saw Michael, I asked if his computer system was working. He said he now had the money to open his own computer company.

" 'If the program is a real hit with companies, what do you think the cost would be for your program?'

"Michael said, 'To begin with, the program will be free. I need to get it into the hands of companies so they can see how great it really is.'

"The second semester was half over, and everyone was talking about Michael being nominated for the Nobel Prize. This was the first time in years anyone from Hebrew

University had been nominated. Michael had changed. He was so busy he had time only for school, and we never saw him or Dr. Messenger except in classes. The solution and artificial skin were selling faster than it could be developed. The credit card company, ICAN, was two weeks away from going nationwide in the U.S. If it was a success, within six months the card would be introduced worldwide. Also, Michael gave his new computer program to five of the largest companies in the world. From what I had heard, they decided not to use anything except his program. They had informed all other companies that supplied them with software that, as of July 1, 2002, all contracts would be null and void. Things were going better for Michael than even he could really imagine.

"Winter was over and the springtime sun was warm on my forehead. Being in Israel in the springtime was a time unlike any place I had ever been. The warm days and cool nights made me think about spring 2,000 years ago. Christ must have thought about spring in the same way I was thinking of it. The only difference was Christ knew this was going to be His last spring. He knew he was going to die for the sins of the world in a very short time.

"I talked to Michael one day when he wasn't so busy. I asked if there was anything special he was working on or doing presently. He said he had read a book about a weapon that was developed in the mid-seventies. The book said it takes low frequency sound waves, shoots them from a special gun, and when they hit something, the target is totally destroyed. The only problem the inventor had was the distance. It could only shoot about 20 feet. The farther the distance, the less impact it had on the object it hit. Michael said if a person could perfect that weapon, it could destroy any object in the world. He said, 'Many nations would pay a pretty dollar to have a weapon like that.'

"I said, 'Just think if a weapon like that was placed in an orbiting satellite.'

"Michael stopped, looked straight at me, and did not say a word for about a minute. He then said, 'You mean the weapon would shoot sound waves from outer space?'

"I said, 'I don't know if it would shoot sound waves or something else.'

"Michael asked, 'What else might be possible?'

" 'I have always toyed with the idea of fire balls. Someone would have to invent something that once it hit the earth's atmosphere, it would ignite into fire.'

"Michael asked, 'Do you have any more ideas?'

"I stood there not saying a word; I had done it again. I said I would not give Michael any ideas, but when he talks or asks questions, I just open up and say what's on my mind.

"May was fast approaching, and things were starting to speed up at the school. Dr. Messenger was flying all over the world every weekend. Sometimes he would take Michael, and sometimes Michael would stay and work on his new laser project. His new laser project was a secret to everyone except Dr. Messenger and myself. Neither one thought for a moment that I knew what the project was. The idea I had given Michael about shooting fire balls from the atmosphere was surely what they were working on. I decided to see if there was anything in the Bible about fire balls coming down from heaven. In Revelation 13:13, it says that 'he doeth great wonders, so that he maketh fire come down from heaven on the earth in the sight of men.' When I read that verse, my heart sank. If Michael is the Antichrist, I had given him the idea about fire balls coming down out of heaven and how to do it. It is, however, the False Prophet that brings the fire balls down from heaven, not the Antichrist, I reminded myself. I believed the False Prophet would use the fire balls to protect the Antichrist. If anyone would try to kill the Antichrist, the False Prophet would consume them with fire from heaven. I said I was not going to form any opinions about Michael, but the evidence continued to mount against him. I would watch to see what Michael did, and if there was a new laser weapon developed or if a new stock exchange company was set up using the name Diabolos, then I would know for certain who Michael was.

"In April Michael asked if I was going back to Oklahoma for the summer. I said I was leaving as soon as school was out.

"He said, 'Remember last year, we had talked about me visiting you this summer?'

"I said, 'I do remember, but I thought with the busy schedule you've had, you would not be able to come to Oklahoma.'

"Michael said, 'I was planning on visiting somewhere around June 12 if that is okay.'

"I told him to be sure and call a day or two ahead of time so I could make plans on different places to go. He said one place he would like to visit was Dallas. (I thought it might be a real treat for Dr. Hale to meet Michael.)

"Michael said, 'Something I have heard a lot about are the rattlesnakes in Oklahoma. The snake hunts, where hundreds of rattlers are captured and killed for steaks, would be a thrill to see.' I told him the snake hunts occur in late April or early May, depending on the weather. By the time we get out of school the hunts would be over. Thank God for that. I'd had enough of rattlesnakes; I didn't want any part of them ever again.

"School would be out in three days, and two whole months of quiet were at hand. Well, I should say seven weeks. One week Michael would be with me. That week could be good or it could be bad. I had no idea which it would be. I had to make sure I treated him like a guest. I knew he didn't have to worry about money. He had so much he could probably never spend it all. In Perry, there weren't a lot of places he could spend money anyway.

"June 10, I received a telephone call from Michael. He said he was in California and would fly into Oklahoma City on the 12th. He planned to rent a car, drive to Perry, and then, if it was all right, we could go to Dallas. I told him I had already made plans at a hotel so we could stay over a couple of nights, and that would give us plenty of time to see all of Dallas.

"On the 12th, Michael drove up in front of my house just before lunch. I asked if he was hungry and he said he was starving. I fixed an old-time hamburger on the grill. After lunch I asked if he was ready to go to Dallas, he said he was. It took about four hours for us to drive to Dallas. We went straight to the hotel and unpacked our bags. Michael said he would like to take a shower before we left to look around Dallas. We took in all the tourist spots of Dallas. When we arrived back at the hotel, we were both exhausted and ready to go to bed. I told him the next day I would introduce him to one of my college professors.

"We were supposed to meet Charlie at his house at four. We arrived a little early just so we could sit back and rest after the previous day. Charlie and Michael seemed to get along pretty well; there were questions and answers and more questions and answers. At five, Charlie told his wife he was going to put the steaks on the grill. I helped Charlie with the steaks and noticed there were six steaks cooking.

"I asked, 'Do you think we're that hungry?'

" 'No,' He chuckled, 'my mother and father are coming over for supper, too.' Within five minutes, his parents showed up. I introduced them to Michael, and they hit it off immediately.

"Michael asked, 'How old are you and Debbie?'

"Tom said with a grin, 'I'm in my eighties and Debbie is, well, she is somewhere around that age also.'

"Michael complimented them on how young they looked. 'Sometime in the future would you be interested in making commercials for me? I have a new idea, and I would need someone in their eighties or nineties.'

" 'Oh, I'll have to think about that if and when the time comes,' Tom said.

" 'If everything works the way it is supposed to work, Tom, I will pay you $250,000 a year.'

"Tom was drinking a glass of water when Michael said how much he would pay him, and I thought Tom would choke to death on the water. He began to cough and cough and cough.

"After he stopped coughing, he said, 'Would you repeat how much you would pay me.'

"Michael said, 'I will pay you one quarter of a million dollars.'

"Without blinking an eye, Tom exclaimed, 'I'll take the job. When do you want me to start?'

"Michael said, 'It could be a year or it could be five years; we are working out the details, and once we have a contract we can start making commercials.'

"The rest of the evening Tom and Michael talked about everything under the sun. It was getting late and I said we must leave. Tom gave Michael his telephone number and said, 'Just call when you want to start the commercials.'

"On the way back to the hotel I asked what kind of commercials Tom and Debbie would be making.

"Michael stated, 'I have interest in a credit card company, and they are wanting to make commercials with elderly people so the senior citizens around the world will not fear credit cards. Most elderly people will not sign up for credit cards, and those who do get them won't use them. We need some strategy to use on the elderly so they will feel comfortable using the card. Tom and Debbie are exactly what I am looking for.'

"The next day we finished touring Dallas and headed back to Oklahoma. I asked if he had been watching the roller coaster ride of the stock market. He said he could not believe how one day the market gains 70 or 80 points and the next day it will lose a couple of hundred.

"I knew I had to ask him, 'What would you do if you owned a stock exchange?' If I didn't ask first, he would ask me and that would give him fuel for more thoughts and ideas.

" 'The first thing I would do is to write a computer program that would stop all transactions if the market started to dip. The second thing is really radical. All investors would have to agree to have more than one account. The third thing I would do is to guarantee that an investor could not lose all he has in one day.' Michael smiled and looked at me and said, 'Thanks.'

"I asked, 'What are you thanking me for?'

"He said, 'I had never thought about owning a stock exchange company.' I had done it again. I said I would not let him ask me what I would do, which would give him ideas. Everything I said would happen was happening. The only remaining thing was the weapon that shoots fire from heaven. I suppose when we get back to school,

Michael will come up to me and say he has just perfected the weapon.

"Michael said I could drop him off at the airport, and the rental company would come and pick up the car he had left at my house. He said he was flying back to California for some important meetings with Dr. Messenger. As the plane lifted off the ground, I thought to myself, 'What if the plane were to crash? I would have been wrong about Michael and my own ideas of who he was would be false.'

"I know I have talked a lot about many things that happened before the rapture. They are very important and essential to understanding how the Antichrist could gain world domination. At this time, I must leave, so I will not let anyone ask questions. All immortals must be in heaven for a special banquet. I will see you tomorrow."

CHAPTER 6

"**THE NOISE WAS** so loud I could not think. There were shouts of anger and I could hear people crying. Others were begging for their lives and saying they would do anything if they would not kill them. The guards walked by my cell and said, 'Your turn will be coming soon.'

"What was I doing here? I had done nothing that would cost me my life. I asked the man in the cell next to mine, 'What is your crime, and do you know what my crime was?'

"The man said, 'Crime? I committed no crime! I am not a criminal!'

"Some of the people the guards were taking said they would conform to the rule, if it meant they would live. One woman asked, 'If you will, take me first. I'm ready to die.' I watched as one by one, men, women and children were being led away.

"One guard said, 'You are going to be next. There is still time, if you want to live.'

"I told the guard, 'I do not understand. What must I do to live?'

"He said, 'All you have to do is to take the number.'

"I asked, 'What number?'

" 'The number of life, 666.'

" 'Did I miss the rapture?'

"The guard came to my cell and opened the door. There were four guards, one on each side of me. We walked out of the ready-made jail that used to be a church, and around one corner. When we circled the corner, I then saw the people standing around and cheering and calling me all kinds of names. I would be next. I had heard the sound, but could not figure out what it was. Then I saw it. It was the first time in my life I had ever seen a guillotine, and now I would have my head cut off just like those ahead of me. The guard asked if I would take the number. I said I would die before I took the number, 666. He said so be it. My hands were tied behind my back. The guards put my head in the holder of the guillotine, and the top of the holder was closed. One guard said I would hear a ringing in my ears when the guillotine blade made the 15-foot drop, and right after that my head would be off. I started to sweat and I was breathing very, very heavily. I heard the ringing, but it would not stop; it kept ringing and ringing. At that time I awoke to the ringing of the telephone. I must have been dreaming, I was sweating and breathing very heavily. Never has a dream seemed so real.

"The call was from my friend in New York. He asked if I had heard the news. I said news about what? He said, 'The ICAN credit card was scheduled to go worldwide in October, but the official report says it is going worldwide in August.'

"I asked if he had read or heard any reports on the usage of the card.

"He said, 'People all over the country are using the card. The commercials are making people believe they really do deserve to buy anything they want. People say they have not seen 8 percent interest on anything in years. Also, with the 5 percent interest on transferred balances, ICAN does not have enough people to process all the apps. Other credit card companies are losing money so quickly, there is fear one or more may go bankrupt within one year if something isn't done.'

"I asked Dan if he still owned stock in the company, and he said he had purchased as much as his billfold could afford.

"I had two days left before I had to leave to go back to Jerusalem. My third year could be my last. I had to do something that would stop Michael. There were so many things that still had to happen. I began to think the situation through. The credit card company was now set up. Michael was talking about forming his own stock exchange company. His computer programs were so sophisticated, one computer friend of mind said he did not understand the language he was using. One area Michael would have a lot of trouble with was the currency of all the nations. The laser weapon that shoots fire from a satellite might be so far-fetched it would never take shape. The only thing that was still disturbing to me was his kindness to the burn children. The Antichrist was not supposed to be kind to anyone. Why would he develop a special solution and artificial skin unless there was something in it for him? It can't be the money. The artificial skin has made him a millionaire, but the credit card company would make him a billionaire many times over.

"The first day of school Michael was not there. I was told he was in Rome doing business. I went to Dr. Messenger's room, but the sub said he was in Babylon. Both were supposed to be back the next day. One boy in my class was a computer genius. I asked if he had ever seen Michael's computer programs. He said he had, but the computer language was something new and he had never seen it before. The day flew by quickly, and before I knew it the day was over. The next day I would talk to Michael and try to find out if he was doing more research on the laser weapon.

"The next day was going very slowly, but I guess it does when you want time to speed up. I wanted my sixth hour to arrive now, but I had two hours remaining until that time. Michael was in my sixth hour class this year, and I was curious about his trip to Rome. Class finally did arrive and I taught as normally as possible, yet anticipating the end when I could visit with Michael. After class I asked Michael, 'How was Rome?'

"He said, 'The city is so beautiful and there are so many historical sites to see one does not know where to start.'

"I told him someone said he was there on business. He chuckled and said, 'You might call it business. I was getting the patent rights for my computer-related writings. The patent rights cover the computer program system, the new program language, the new computer games, the new user violation codes, and the new computer company I have just formed.'

" 'Have you had any luck with the laser sound weapon?'

"He said, 'That has been put on the back burner at this time, but it will become functional very soon.' The more questions I asked the less information he gave. He then told me he did not have the time to tell me any more about his trip. I asked Michael if he would like to come over for supper and tell me everything about the patents and how it will impact the world. He said he would be over at six.

"We ate at six and later sat down to talk. Michael began telling me of Rome and the sites he had seen and how he would love to live there some day. He said, 'The city is so rich in history, and to be in the city that had conquered the known world was a real thrill.' He told me about the international patents he receive for all of his hard work. 'The computer program system will replace all systems within five years.' He said he needed the patent so pirates could not steal him blind. 'The new adult games and children computer games will change the way people look at and play computer games.'

"I stopped him and asked if he could give me details of what he was speaking about. 'I know nothing of computers, and the more detail you give me the more I can understand what you are saying.'

"Michael said he would start all over and make it easy for me to understand. Michael first started with his computer program system. He explained how systems work and how some companies prefer one system over another. He said his system works totally different than all others. 'My system requires that when you first learn my program, one must put on the head phones and watch the video. The program teacher begins telling the person how to use the system. In the program teacher, there are subliminal messages that enhance the learning ability of the individual. There are 20 videos that have three one-hour segments. Each video is loaded with subliminal messages. The subliminal messages activate the subconscious and motivate the person to over-achieve in whatever he or she is working on. I can take an average person, use the videos and head phones on them, and when they are finished with the course, they will have a working knowledge of the system that far exceeds someone else who did not use my system of teaching. You see, Professor Wilson, it is not the computer program that is so sophisticated and user friendly, it is the method of teaching the system and opening the mind to knowledge that is dormant.

" 'The computer games will require a helmet that is

similar to virtual reality helmets. The difference is price. The computer game and helmet will cost $100. Virtual reality helmets alone cost between $300 to $400.

" 'The violation codes are very unique. Many people will buy a program, load it in their computer and let a friend load it in their computer, which is a crime. When the program is first loaded, the violation code reads the internal serial number of the computer and puts it in memory in the program disk. The program disk is required to be in the computer when the computer is turned on. The disk reads the internal serial number to verify that it is the same serial number that was installed the very first time. The program will not operate if the serial number is different. If a person were to buy a new computer, they would have to call our 800 number to have a new code for their program. The new program language I invented is called VEAL. It stands for Voice Electronic Analytic Language.'

"Michael said, 'It is a new computer language that uses voice recognition to write programs. You speak into the microphone and tell the computer what you want. Within minutes it is done.' He said all programers will use this language in the near future.

"Michael stated he needed to be under the umbrella of a company, so he set up his own computer company. He said he would put all computer companies out of business within ten years.

"I thought to myself, 'With what he has now, the only person who may go out of business is Michael.'

"The next day I went by Dr. Messenger's room to see how his trip was to Babylon. He said since Iraq started to rebuild the ancient city of Babylon many investors are looking at Babylon to invest in. 'Babylon will be a very important city in the very near future.' The more we talked the more I started to see a different side of Dr. Messenger. He was telling me about the Tower of Babel and how the world had almost had one religion. 'If it is possible, Babylon will again be the place where one religion will be worldwide.'

"I asked Dr. Messenger if he really believed what he had just said. 'I believe it so much I am going to move my headquarters to Babylon!' "

I decided I would stop and see if anyone would like to ask a question. I had to leave so quickly yesterday, I did not take any questions. I asked if there were any questions.

"Andy, you have a question?"

"Yes, Brother Steven. Yesterday you said you had to go to a banquet. What kind of banquet did you go to, and does the Bible tell of this banquet?"

"The Bible does not tell of this banquet. This banquet is held every month in heaven. Even though there is no time in heaven, it would be equal to your time on earth. We worship Christ with our hearts and with our singing. The banquet is a time of fellowshipping and praising the Lamb.

"Wanda, what is your question?"

"Sometimes you think that Michael was the Antichrist and other times you didn't. Could you explain?"

"The things Michael did and what he said made me believe he was the Antichrist, while other times I doubted that we Christians would know who the Antichrist would be before the rapture. The things that were being set up by Michael, such as the credit card company, the stock market company, the development of artificial skin, the computer programs and maybe a laser sound weapon could be used by the real Antichrist when he came on the scene. Perhaps Michael was the person who put everything together and the real Antichrist would manipulate them away from Michael. It could be the Antichrist might have had Michael killed for his inventions. I did not know if Michael was the Antichrist or if the Antichrist was still in the future. As a Christian, we should not judge a person unless we are absolutely sure what we believe is true."

There were so many questions I knew it could take hours to answer them all. The questions were coming from the people who were born in the millennium. The ones who became Christians during the tribulation had not asked one question. It may be too painful to think of that terrible time on earth when more than half the population died. The famines, the wars, the droughts and the starvation made people re-evaluate how precious life really is. Those who went through the tribulation know how difficult life was each day. No one knew if it would be their last day or maybe the next day would be their last. The only thing that was certain was, if you were a Christian and you died, you knew exactly where you were going.

"Jerry, you have a question?"

"A week ago you said the Antichrist gave people the number 666; why?"

"When the Antichrist signed the peace treaty with Israel, that signing began the seven-year tribulation. The exact date was April 3, 2011. That date is very important because exactly three and one-half years from that date, the Antichrist would go into the rebuilt tribulation temple, sit on the throne and proclaim himself to be God. At that time the Antichrist required everyone who accepted him as God to take his number, 666, to show they did believe he was God. If a person took the number, he or she would be doomed for eternity. One reason the Jews knew the Antichrist was not God was because the Antichrist entered the temple on October 3, 2014, one of the most holy days in Israel, Yom Kippur. They knew the true God would not enter on a holy day, and also the true God would not have to proclaim himself to be God; his prophets, his angels, and the Bible would proclaim who the true God was. And the Bible did exactly that.

"The Bible states, in the Book of Daniel, what was about to happen. The Bible also said at the end of the tribulation Jesus would come back and destroy all those armies that have gathered to make war. The Bible tells us who God is. In the Gospel of John, Chapter 1, Verse 1, it says, 'In the beginning was the Word, and the Word was with God, and the Word was God.' Also in verse 14 it says, 'And the Word was made flesh, and dwelt among us (and we beheld his glory, the glory as of the only begotten of the Father), full of grace and truth.' There is only one person these two verses are talking about, and that is Jesus Christ. Jesus was the Word and he was made flesh.

"Before the rapture, many people did not believe in Jesus or the Bible, but when the tribulation began, there were a multitude of people that believed. During the last 3-1/2 years of the tribulation, a person had to have the number 666 in order to buy, trade or have a job. The Antichrist controlled every aspect of the world economy. The things I have told you about which were being set up by Michael were the beginnings of the control of the world's economy. I did not know for certain at that time, but I had a feeling that somehow they could be used as the primary means of world power.

"At this time I will continue telling what happened before the rapture, and you may ask more questions when I am finished.

"Michael was a junior in the fall of 2002. The grades that he made were beyond words. Every test he took, every paper he wrote and every assignment and class project he was involved with was perfect. As a matter of fact, when he graduated, he was the only student in the history of Hebrew University who had a perfect score on everything. Michael never missed one question on a test, and he never had a paper that was grammatically incorrect. Hebrew University was given an anonymous $100-million gift the year Michael graduated. I had a good idea where the money had come from, but no one else had any idea who would give the school that much money.

"By the time Michael graduated he was a secret billionaire. His credit card company had already put one credit card company out of business. There were only four major credit card companies left in the world, and Michael's main goal was to put them out of business also. He bought one square block of land in Rome. That would be the new location of his stock exchange company. The building of the new stock exchange started in March of 2003, and it took three years to finish. The grand opening was March 13, 2006. Dignitaries from all over the world came to the opening. It was billed as the only stock exchange in the world where an investor could not lose all his money in one day.

"The name was kept secret until the day of the grand opening. There was a large sheet covering the name, and when Michael finished his speech, he said he would remove the sheet to reveal the name. When Michael pulled the sheet, the name was revealed. I could not believe what I saw. The name was the 'Global Stock Exchange.'

"I thought back to a dream Michael had shared with the class about a man telling him of a stock exchange company that Michael would own and how the name would be the Global Stock Exchange. Michael had put a lot of thought into his new company. He wrote a program that would stop all transactions if there was a 100-point drop. By having all business stopped if there was a 100-point drop, it would ensure that no one could lose all their money in one day. He also required all investors to have two or more accounts. For example, if a person opened an account and wanted to buy only IBM stock, he was forbidden. An investor had to have two accounts, one for IBM and another for some other stock. The investor also had to have equal shares of each stock. Michael said by having half of one's money in one stock and half in another, there would be no way they would ever go bankrupt.

"Not only did the plan work, but it started to hurt other stock exchanges. The rumors of unfair trades, stock manipulations, executive infighting and brokers who were cheating the customers brought the fall of all stock exchanges in the world by the end of 2009.

"During Michael's senior year, he had been working very had at something secret. No one knew what he was working on except Dr. Messenger. Michael had purchased a building in southern Jerusalem where he and Dr. Messenger worked most weekends and three or four nights a week until midnight. In December of 2004 the news was released to the news media of a new laser weapon.

"The weapon used low-pitch sound to destroy any object it hit and at any distance. Michael had talked the British government into giving him an old ship that was supposed to be destroyed by the British navy. The ship was taken out to sea some 1,000 miles from Israel. Michael typed in the coordinate numbers where the ship was, and fired. Within five minutes, the ship was destroyed by the laser sound wave. Michael thought it was a great invention, but the nations of the world did not think that way. The Arab nations did not know if Michael would give the new weapon to Israel or what he would do. Also, Israel did not know what Michael would do. Would he sell the new weapon to the highest bidder, or would he attempt to blackmail a country into thinking his way? At one point the Israeli Masad had decided to have him assassinated, but the plan was mysteriously revealed to the media, and those involved were jailed. Michael was becoming one of the most important men in the world.

"Because of the uproar of his new weapon, in 2005 he founded the "Brotherhood of Human Reasoning." The goal of the Brotherhood was to reason things out in a peaceful manner. The cost to join the Brotherhood was $100,000 . What the money bought was time, in case a country was about to go to war with another country. Michael would go and negotiate a peace treaty between the countries. His first test came right after 80 nations signed up to belong to the Brotherhood. India and China had border fights over a small piece of land. Michael went immediately to Burma and met with both parties, and resolved the crisis in two days. After the China crisis, almost all the other countries joined the Brotherhood.

"Michael continued to resolve disputes between nations, until he was known as the 'Prince of Peace.' The newspaper headlines and the news medias would state, 'The Prince of Peace has brought peace to two more countries that were on the verge of fighting.' Michael's slogan was, 'Everything can be worked out in a peaceable manner.' By the end of 2009 Michael was the most popular and important man in the world. He was acclaimed as the most likely person to be the president of the world, if a position like that ever came about.

"Those of you who went through the tribulation know who the Antichrist was and what he did. Those of you who were never told the story of the tribulation or who the Antichrist was have no idea what his name was. It is best to reveal who the Antichrist was and what he did to humanity. The Antichrist was Michael D. Glispbe, and the False Prophet was Dr. Paul A. Messenger. These two men made up two-thirds of the false trinity. The other third was the Devil himself. The things Michael did in order to take control of the world were monstrous. Dr. Messenger did everything in his power to put Michael into the position of the Antichrist. People were murdered in order to take over companies and to accelerate Michael into the world's eye. Dr. Messenger knew the time was near, so he set up the World Council of Religious Beliefs. The idea was to get everyone together for the one world religion during the tribulation period. God was letting these two work and pull everything together to get things ready for the tribulation. The false trinity was only a matter of years from becoming a reality."

THE EARLY YEARS OF MICHAEL D. GLISPBE

And I stood upon the sand of the sea, and saw a beast rise up out of the sea, having seven heads and ten horns, and upon his horns ten crowns, and upon his heads the name of blasphemy.

Revelation 13:1

CHAPTER 7

"**NOW THAT** I have told you who the Antichrist is, I am sure there are questions you are wanting to ask, so you may now ask questions.

"Bonnie, what is your question?"

"Since the Antichrist is Michael, you stated one time before that he hated his parents. Could you give us the reason why a son would hate his parents?"

"I guess it's best to start at the beginning and give you the details before Michael was born and his early years until he entered college. This way you can truly understand the circumstances of Michael's life.

"Michael's grandmother, Kim, was born in an orthodox Jewish home in Ireland. Her parents were very strict and would not let her date until she was 18 years old. She had met many young Jewish men that she liked, but none seemed to spark the fire women look for when they are looking for a husband. One day while walking home she met a young, dark and very handsome man by the name of Omar. Omar walked her most of the way home, but when she entered the Jewish area, he stopped and said he had forgotten to get something for his mother, and rushed off. After going 30 foot, he turned and yelled, 'Can I see you tomorrow?'

"Kim said she would meet him at the park at five.

"The next day he was there and they sat and talked for almost an hour. He asked if she was Jewish and she said, 'Yes, very orthodox.'

"She asked if he was Arab, and he told her no. He stated he was part Spanish.

"Every day they would meet and talk, and on Friday or Saturday they would go to the local soda store and have a coke or something else. They continued to see each other for a year, until one day he asked if she would marry him. He said shyly, 'Maybe it is best that you wait until I tell you something before you say yes.' At that time he dropped an atomic bomb.

"He said, 'I am not part Spanish, but Arab.'

"Kim began to cry and said, 'I do not know what I am going to do.' If she said she would marry him, her family would cast her out for defiling herself and the family name. But she loved him so much, she was between a rock and a hard spot. She decided her love for him was so great she would marry him anyway. She made him promise not to tell anyone he was Arab. Omar agreed and said he would continue to say he was Spanish.

"Omar and Kim were married in 1942. Omar and Kim were so happy, the only way possible to show their love even more was by having a baby. Six months after they were married, Kim became pregnant. The happy time only lasted for one day. On Omar's way home, a car went out of control, hit him broadside, and Omar was killed. Kim was devastated. She did not know where to turn or what to do. She did not have a job and there was no insurance. She had but one choice and that was to go back home. Omar was one to plan ahead, so he always had the rent paid two months in advance. Kim was almost four months pregnant and desperate.

"One day, a young man came around the corner of the grocery store and bumped into her. He said he was sorry, but then 'Whoa, maybe I'm not sorry after all!'

"Kim looked at him and said, 'What do you mean?'

"Andrew Brian Glispbe replied, 'If I was sorry for bumping into the most beautiful woman I've laid eyes on, I would have to be crazy, so I'm not sorry.'

"He asked, 'Are you buying a lot?' and she told him just a few items.

"He asked, 'May I carry your groceries home for you?' She decided there would be nothing wrong in that so she agreed.

"On the way home they talked, and Kim told him of the death of her husband and that she was pregnant. Andrew considered her the most beautiful woman he had ever seen and asked if he could see her again? They continued to meet and became friends. Within three months, Andrew asked her to marry him. They were married in two weeks. In less than two months Kim had a baby boy. Andrew said he wanted the baby to have his name, even though it was half Arab. They named the baby Tony Andrew.

"Before Andrew met Kim, he was going to night college and had but one year remaining in order to get his degree. Plans changed now that he had a family. It would take at least two or maybe three years to get the degree, but he would not quit.

"Two years later Andrew received his degree. With a degree it would open up many avenues that had been closed. One of Andrew's friends worked for the government. He told Andrew that he could get him on if he wanted to change careers.

"Andrew did change, and one thing lead to another. Soon, Andrew had received notice that he would be the new head of the department. Andrew never dreamed he would ever be in politics, but there he was. The years went by quickly and soon their son, Tony Andrew, would be out of school and looking for a job.

"Tony decided working for the government, like his father, was not a bad job. He went to college, and while at college he met a young girl by the name of Shannon. After dating for two years, they decided to get married. Tony's mother had taught him how to speak in Hebrew while he was growing up, as well as the Jewish customs. When Tony decided to get married, his mother, Kim, reminded him when the Jewish holidays rolled around, they expected him to come over to their house. Even though Andrew did not align with this faith, he went along, just to keep peace in the family.

"Tony and Shannon were married in May and went to the race track for their honeymoon. They both were avid race fans. They loved to watch the horses run and they also liked winning. You could find them at the track every Saturday, regardless of the weather. Tony did not have a very good paying job. He still needed one year in order to get his degree. Sometimes they did not have enough money to go to the race track to place bets or even to watch, so they would listen on the radio to hear the results.

"After getting paid one day, Tony came home and gave the money to Shannon and told her to buy enough food to last them for two weeks. The next day, instead of buying food, Shannon went to the race track and decided she would put all the money on a long shot. The horse's name was Diabolos. He had a 100 to 1 shot to win. Shannon knew she shouldn't use the money on betting, because they had not won on a horse for three months, and that was all the money they had. She reasoned that if the horse wins, then they would win 10,000 pounds. At that time, a pound was worth more than an American dollar. Diabolos had lost six races in a row. The only reason he was in this race was they needed a fast horse to set the pace. Diabolos had led all six races until he reached the half-way mark, and that was when he ran out of speed. Shannon put all the money on Diabolos and then found a place to sit and watch the race. When the gates opened, Diabolos went to the front of the pack. Shannon said to herself, 'One-fourth of the way around and still in first place.' Diabolos continued to lead and Shannon said, 'Halfway around and still in first place.' She knew what had happened in the other six races at the half-way marker, but this day was different. Diabolos seemed to be running harder and faster at the halfway marker. As Diabolos raced down the back straight away, instead of just leading, he was pulling away from the second-place horse. Shannon was on her feet yelling and screaming at the top of her lungs for Diabolos. With 300 yards to go, Diabolos was ahead by 12 lengths! The other horses tried to make a last-minute run, but he was too far ahead. At the window, the man asked how she would like to have the money? She said, 'In cash,' and then she began laughing.

"After leaving the race track, she stopped and bought everything she wanted at the store. When Tony walked in the door, he could not believe the smell in the house. It was the smell of steak! Shannon explained what had happened and that she would put the rest of the money in the bank the next day.

"The next time Diabolos was supposed to race was in three weeks. This time, Tony and Shannon would go and watch the race together. The newspaper said Diabolos just got lucky, and for him to have another race like the one he previously won would be a miracle. Tony and Shannon bought tickets and sat up high, so they could see the whole race. The horses were placed in the gates and when the gates were opened, Diabolos was in front again. Being a 50 to 1 long shot to win seemed strange, since he was leading the pack. Things would not be the same after this race. Diabolos won his second race and he would never be a long shot again. Diabolos continued to win every race he ran. It was then that his owner decided to ship him to the United States to try and win the Triple Crown. If he could win the Triple Crown, he would be the first in the history of Ireland to do so.

"Diabolos arrived in America four months before the first stage of the Triple Crown. The cool climate of Ireland could be a factor in the race unless he became accustomed to the humidity and warmer temperatures. Each day Diabolos worked out, the more it seemed the climate enhanced his speed. Three days before the race, his time broke the track record. The trainer and owner knew the day of the race would be a day that would go down in history.

"The newspapers were saying how Diabolos had not run against the quality of horses which the U.S. produced. The odds for Diabolos to win were 10 to 1. The favored horse was Watch My Tail. He had not lost a race in his career and the other horses were, as his name implied, watching his tail. He was a 2 to 1 favorite. Tony and Shannon decided, since they had not had a real honeymoon, it might be nice to go to the Kentucky Derby. The money they had saved from the other races gave them a nest egg for the future. They would bet $2,000 on Diabolos to win.

"Tony and Shannon were seated in their booths awaiting the race like all the other people. There was an excitement in the air and a feeling that history was about to be made. It took 10 minutes to get the horses into the gates. As soon as the last horse was in the gate, they opened the gates and out came the horses, with Diabolos leading. Around the first turn he was one length ahead of all the others. Diabolos had gained a little on the curve, and going down the straight away he had two lengths on the others and was pulling away. Going around the last curve he was a full five lengths ahead of the second place horse, Watch My Tail. All that was left was the straightaway to the finish line. Both jockeys were hitting their horses and doing everything possible to make them go faster. Watch My Tail was gaining on Diabolos, and with 200 yards to go it was an even race. At that point Diabolos must have reached down and pulled up his reserve energy. In the last 200 yards he drove ahead and won by three lengths. Everyone said they had never seen anything like it in the history of racing. The newspapers wrote about the power that was stored in the horse and were now predicting him to win the Triple Crown. Tony and Shannon won $20,000.

"On their flight back to Ireland, they could not believe how lucky they had been, betting on Diabolos. Shannon asked Tony, 'If we were to have children, what names would you like?' They talked about girl names and then boy names, but there were none that appealed to them. Shannon told Tony they had better come up with some names soon.

"Tony's eyes started to get bigger and bigger and a smile came on his face. 'Are you telling me you are going to have a baby?'

" 'Yes, and we need to find a name for our baby.'

"Tony said, 'I'm wondering if the name Michael would be a good name.'

"Shannon said, 'That sounds good to me. We have made a lot of money on Diabolos, why don't we name him Michael Diabolos?'

"Tony thought about the names and confirmed, 'Michael Diabolos is what it will be, if it is a boy. If it is a girl, we will name her Beth Diana.'

"Back in Ireland, Tony and Shannon could not believe their luck. They knew they had two races to go, and if Diabolos continued to run the way he had, they would be set for life. Each day came and went until it was time for them to fly back to the U.S.

"The Preakness would be the next test for Diabolos. If he won The Preakness, there was only one race to go, the Belmont. Diabolos had won Tony and Shannon $20,000 at the Kentucky Derby, so they decided they would bet it all. Diabolos was a 3 to 1 favorite.

"The day of the race, they thought they had made a mistake because it was raining. The track would be slow and that would give the other horses a chance. The horses were placed in the gates, and then they were off. The race was over almost before it was started. Around the first turn, Diabolos was ahead by one length. Then it happened. The second-place horse slipped on the mud and went down. It was a chain reaction! Horse after horse went down. Out of the 12 horses racing, there were only five left in the race. Diabolos won by 11 lengths. Now there was but one race to go. If Diabolos could just win that race, they would never be in need of money again.

"Time was flying by so fast, the Belmont was only a week away. They both were ready to go, but Shannon starting getting sick every morning. Her doctor said it might be best if she got her rest and did not fly until after the baby was born. Tony agreed, and on Thursday, he would make his last trip to America alone.

"Tony put everything he had won from the last two races on Diabolos to win. The newspapers were saying he had a very good chance of winning the Triple Crown, if he did not get out too fast and falter at the end. The horses were placed in the gates. On the left of Diabolos was Watch My Tail. 'This race might be one that people would talk about for years,' thought Tony. When the gates were opened, Diabolos and Watch My Tail were side by side. Around the first turn, they stayed side by side, and also down the straight-away. The other horses were eight lengths back and fading. Both jockeys were playing a mind game against each other. They knew what their horses could do. It was just a matter of time until one made a move. As they rounded the last curve, both horses were still running side by side. With less than a 100 feet to go, Diabolos moved up by a head. The photo finish showed the winner was Diabolos. He had just won the Triple Crown.

"Most of the money Tony and Shannon had won was placed in an account that would pay them a specific amount of money each month. They also had placed enough money in a trust so their children could go to college. When it came time for Shannon to give birth, there was excitement on both sides of the family. Kim said, 'I am going to teach my grandchild how to speak Hebrew and all the customs of the Jewish people.' Shannon's father wanted to teach him or her how to hunt.

"The day came when Shannon told Tony it was time to go to the hospital. At 10:22 she gave birth to a baby boy, Michael Diabolos Glispbe. Neither Tony or Shannon would know how their son would hate the name they had given to him.

"Tony worked while Shannon stayed home with their newborn son. They both loved to be near their son and watch when he did things that all newborn babies do. There was something different about their baby. They could never put their finger on what it was; there was just something different. Most babies will try to say Mama or Dada at the age of 12 to 15 months. Michael was saying those words at nine months. When Michael was 10 months old, Shannon told Tony she was going to have another baby. Tony was more excited about a second baby than he was the first. He said he had always wanted a large family, maybe six or seven children. 'The more kids, the more I get excited and the more love I can give. How soon will it be before the baby arrives?'

"Shannon said, 'I am three months pregnant.'

"The days went by slower this time than they had with Michael. Shannon had to take care of Michael and watch what she was doing so she wouldn't hurt her unborn child. Kim was coming over to the house almost every day. She would rock Michael to sleep and whisper in his ear Hebrew words. By the time Michael was one year old, he was putting words together to form sentences. He could also tell colors and he knew how to count from 1 to 5. Kim never told Tony or Shannon, but she knew Michael was a gifted child. She kept it to herself, and when she would babysit, she was always speaking in Hebrew. She would also write numbers on a little chalk board and make him do everything left-handed. She believed that children who were left-handed would use more of their brain than right-handed children.

"Shannon called Kim and told her she thought that it was time for her to go to the hospital. Shannon asked Kim to take Michael back to her house until she returned from the hospital? Kim said she would be right over, and not to worry about a thing. Kim picked Michael up, and on the way back to her house she told Michael that he was going to be a very great man some day.

"At 16 months, Michael was putting sentences together and talking more like an adult than a baby. Whenever Michael would go to his grandparents' house, Kim would always put on classical music and make Michael sit and listen. She would tell him the name of the songs, and next time he heard the song he knew the name. When Michael was one year old, Andrew purchased a small piano. Kim knew how to play the piano, so at the age of 13 months she began to let Michael tap on the keys. She started to put notes together to make small tunes for Michael. Within one month Michael could remember the tunes and play them without looking at the keyboard. Michael was always asking if he could play the piano. The night Kim took Michael home while Shannon was going to the hospital was no different. Michael would play the songs he loved. If he did not like a song, he would not play it.

"That night, Michael's baby brother was born. Tony and Shannon did not have any names picked out as they had for Michael.

"One of the nurses walked in and said, 'It is really a sunny day today.'

"Shannon looked at Tony and said, 'That is what we will name him, Sonny.' Their new son would be called Sonny William Glispbe.

"When Tony and Shannon brought Sonny home, Michael watched Sonny all the time. Michael would tickle his feet and kiss him on the belly, which made Sonny laugh. At night, Michael would cry if he could not be in the same room with his baby brother. Tony had to have their beds together so Michael could look at Sonny. Michael would also speak to Sonny in Hebrew.

"Michael was so intelligent, he was working math problems at two years of age. Kim would come over two or three times a week. She would take Michael on long walks and talk in Hebrew and teach him poetry. Kim started doing the same thing with Sonny as she had done with Michael. When she rocked him, she would talk to him in Hebrew. She would also take things out of his right hand and put them into his left hand. Sonny was not the gifted child that Michael was; however, Sonny was an average child.

"When Sonny was one year old, Shannon let everyone know that number three was on the way. She said she was four months along and she was hoping that it would be a girl. Tony and Shannon decided they would look at names before this baby was born. The two names they picked were Clint Daniel, just in case another boy arrived, and if it was a girl, she would be named Mary Beth.

"Shannon was having problems with this child, and the doctor told her it would probably be her last. Shannon was sick most of the time and was afraid she would lose the baby before it was born. When she was in her ninth month, she was sure she could have the baby. At the hospital, the doctor had to take the baby by cesarean section. They named the baby Mary Beth. Tony and Shannon had three kids, 33 months, 17 months, and a newborn. They had their hands full, but there were no complaints.

"At night, Michael would watch Sonny and Mary Beth sleep. He seemed to be fascinated by his brother and sister. When Sonny was a month old, Michael would say, 'My baby.' Michael loved his brother and sister so much he did not want to be away from them for more than 10 minutes.

"One day Shannon called Kim and asked if Michael could come over for the night. She said the other two kids were sick and she was afraid they would give it to Michael. Michael did not want to go, but Kim told him he had to go or he would get sick also.

"At 2 o'clock in the morning, fire trucks could be heard coming down the street. Tony and Shannon's house was on fire. The fire was so intense, it had started the house that was next to it on fire. The firemen were told that a whole family was still inside. One fireman took an axe and was able to break in the front door. One fireman went in and was able to find Sonny and bring him out. His body was lifeless. They poured a special solution over his burns to try and stop the pain. The fire was so hot if anyone else went inside, they might not come out. One fireman decided he would go in and maybe he would get lucky and find the other child or one of the parents. Before he was able to come out, the roof collapsed, trapping him inside with all the others. The fire took four lives that night. Sonny hung on for almost three days, but infection set in, and on the fourth day after the fire, he died. Michael was the only one left. Andrew and Kim said they would raise him as their own son. The money Tony had put away would be used for Michael's education and also for expenses he would have when he got older.

"Every day Kim would talk to Michael in Hebrew and tell him how God let his family die. She said it was all God's fault. She told Michael if God was a loving God he would not have let those things happen to them. She said she would never have anything to do with God again. Michael asked Kim if God took Sonny and Mary Beth. She said he did and it was not right. Michael wanted to know how God took them.

"Kim said, 'God used a fire to burn them and that caused them to die.'

"Michael would always say, 'Fire is bad, God is bad.' When Michael was five, he saw Andrew light a match and start a fire. At that time, Michael told his grandpa that he should put the fire out before he caught the house on fire. Michael thought if there was fire that a house would be burned down. Michael also associated fire with pain and death. As the years went by, Michael never lost his fear of fire.

"In the area where Andrew and Kim lived, there was a small community of Jewish families. They had their own store, school, bakery and a synagogue. Everyone in the community knew where the Jewish areas started, and unless a person had business there, they stayed out. The Jews never felt like outcasts. They held jobs, went to other stores to shop and just acted normal.

"Some of the Jewish boys went to the public school, but they were always being harassed. When Michael started school at the age of six, no one expected trouble in the Jewish school. Well, there was trouble from day one. When the day started, the teacher would call out the children's names so the other children would get to know one another. When she got to Michael, she introduced him as Michael Diabolos Glispbe. The other children started to laugh and said, 'He is not Jewish. Who ever heard of a Jew named Glispbe?' That whole day he was taunted and ridiculed for not being Jewish. It was one thing to be Jewish and go to the public school, but it was a whole new ball game if you are not Jewish in the eyes of the other children and you go to a Jewish school.

"The next day, Kim went to school with Michael and had a talk with his teacher and explained that she was Jewish and that Michael's father was half Jewish. 'Even though Michael is not full Jewish, he is one quarter, and as long as he lives in my house he will attend the Jewish school.'

"All through the first grade, Michael was teased and made fun of because he was not a Jew in the eyes of the other children. During that first year, Michael far surpassed the other children in everything he did in class. As a matter of fact, he considered it very boring to attend school.

"He said, 'There is not a challenge, everything is so easy.' Kim talked Andrew into letting Michael attend another school when the regular school was over each afternoon, even though it would cost more. There was an elderly Jewish man by the name of Joshua Cohen who had set up a special school for children who wanted and needed extra help. Kim explained that Michael was a gifted child and what he needed was a challenge. Mr. Cohen said he would see just how gifted Michael was.

"The first day Michael showed him he did not need help in any subject, he needed a challenge. Mr. Cohen started with math. Michael did all the problems and asked for more. Within one hour, Michael was solving algebra problems. That first night proved to be what Michael needed.

"Mr. Cohen would give Michael the challenge he needed. Michael learned physics, chemistry and all the higher levels in every subject which Mr. Cohen could think of.

"The Jewish school was another story. One day, one of the boys told Michael he was the Devil. Michael did not say anything; he just thought the boy was teasing him. But when the boy said the Devil's name was Diabolos, that was when Michael fought back. He hit the boy and knocked him on the ground and jumped on top of him and continued to hit him until he had blood coming from his nose, mouth and forehead. Michael told him to never say that to him again. Michael was in a fight almost every week. The boys would call him the Devil, and Michael would fight back. For a boy in the first grade to be in a fight almost every week was unbelievable. The teasing never stopped.

"One day Michael told a group of boys that one day he would get back at all of them. He said he was going to make them pay, and pay dearly for being so cruel to him. Michael did not have any friends in school. The boys did not like him, and if any girl did like him, they knew that the other children would make fun of them. Michael made friends with a couple of boys who went to the public school. They did not care if he was Jewish or if he was not Jewish. They liked Michael.

"Mr. Cohen worked with Michael so much and taught him so much that the teachers asked Andrew and Kim if they could push Michael ahead one year in school. The teachers said he was so much more advanced than the other children, the school was boring to him. Kim did not want to push Michael ahead. She thought it may harm him more than help him. Michael was never advanced forward in school.

"The years went by quickly, and before anyone knew it Michael was in junior high. The boys continued to call him the Devil and say he was not Jewish. In a rage, Michael said, 'One day I will get even with all the Jews. Since you say I am not Jewish, then I denounce my Jewish heritage and become your enemy.'

"From that day forward Michael decided in his heart he would get even. He thought back when he was little and remembered his brother and sister dying in the fire and how his grandmother said it was God who let it happen. He said, 'Since God let my family die and the Jews are God's people, then God is my enemy also.' Michael started to look at things a lot differently than he had ever looked at things before.

"Hatred never left Michael. He hated the name his

parents had given him. He hated all Jews except his grandmother and Mr. Cohen. He hated God and anything that was Godly. Michael would say, 'God is so cruel; he has no heart, and if he did have a heart how could he let bad things happen to good people? What did my mother or father do or my brother and sister do to deserve death? They were good, but an unloving and cruel God killed them. He killed my people and one day I will kill his people.' Michael began reading about Adolph Hitler and the way he had tried to exterminate the Jewish population. The more he read, the more intriguing the material was. Every spare minute he was reading about the death camps Hitler had set up and the different methods that were used to take the lives of the Jews. Michael's heart was turning hard toward God and the things of God. There was nothing that could be done for Michael. He was lost, totally lost.

"The Bible says a person can only harden their heart to a point and if they go beyond that point, then God will harden their heart. Michael had gone beyond that point. From then on, God was hardening Michael's heart and preparing him for the mission that Michael was destined to take. The Antichrist was alive and well on planet earth.

"When Michael started high school, things changed a little. Some of the boys grew up and stopped teasing him, but others continued with the slurs and the mocking. What hurt Michael more than the teasing and slurs was that the girls did not want anything to do with him. Michael wanted to be like the other guys and have a girl friend, but the girls knew what would happen if they were to date him.

"The rest of his high school years went by quickly and were uneventful. When it came time for him to go to college, Kim suggested Hebrew University in Jerusalem.

Michael was against Hebrew University from the very start. But as Michael thought about going there, he decided, 'What better way to learn about the Jewish people than to be where they are.'

"I have told you about his four years at the university, but the things that would occur after he left the university, I have not told you about. In the following days, I will tell you how ruthless he became, and how he turned into a liar and a murderer."

CHAPTER 8

"**I SAID** I would tell you about the years after Michael graduated, but if there are any questions, I will answer them first.

"Clay, what is your question?"

"When you are telling us of the things that occurred before the rapture, are you telling us as if it is first-hand knowledge, exactly like it happened, or are you using hindsight?"

"Sometimes I am using first-hand knowledge, and other times I am using hindsight, while other times I am using the knowledge that I received when I was given my incorruptible body. I don't think it is necessary or important for you to know if it is first-hand, hindsight, or if it is information I am now conscious about. What I am telling you is the truth about the actual events. I will answer more questions later.

"May 20, 2004, Michael D. Glispbe graduated from Hebrew University. As I had told you previously, Michael was a billionaire when he graduated. Everything was going as planned. He and Dr. Messenger were manipulating, lying and using unscrupulous tactics to advance their goals. Dr. Messenger was not looking for any praise or acclamation for himself; he wanted all of that for Michael. Many things Dr. Messenger did, he would say Michael had done. This way Michael was the one in the limelight and the one who people were looking at. As the days went by, it was Michael who was gaining in popularity and becoming known all over the world.

"The credit card company which Michael set up was making him so much money he would never be able to spend it all. Rumors swirled about the remaining credit card companies in the world. One rumor stated that the two largest credit card companies were going to merge and put ICAN out of business. It did not put ICAN out of business. It made people use their card more for fear the rumors were true. The more the ICAN card was used, the less the other cards were being used. The other four companies had assets far beyond the assets of ICAN. However, ICAN was moving up fast, but not as fast as Michael wanted.

"Michael put together two new plans that would bring on the downfall of the other companies. The first thing Michael did was to give all customers a one-month grace period on the interest. When the billing went out in November, there would be no interest charged for December. In other words, a customer only paid interest 11 months out of the year. The second plan was to put the maximum limit on all cards at $200,000, in the event a person wanted to buy a new home. Also, by using the ICAN card to purchase a new home, he or she would not need a large down payment. The card covered everything.

"If a person bought regular items, the interest would be the same as before, but if a person wanted to buy a house, the interest rate would drop to 6 percent. The plan worked to perfection. The people who could not afford to buy a new home because of the large down payment could now have their own home. Six percent interest for buying a house had not been seen since way back in 1969. Homes that Realtors could not sell were selling so quickly they had more people wanting to buy homes than were available. Builders were building homes as fast as they could. The boom was not only in the United States, but all over the world. The ICAN credit card made it possible for people everywhere to buy the things that were only a dream before.

"Michael and Dr. Messenger contacted one of their friends who had ties to the underworld in New York. They needed some work done for them, and if the people in New York would do the work, it would pay $500,000, no questions asked and no traces should be left. The next day, their friend said his friends in New York would take the job, no questions asked. James J. Lucas was the person the New York group was supposed to eliminate. Mr. Lucas was the CEO of the largest of the four remaining credit card companies in the world.

"James J. Lucas was one of those men who always kept everything exact. On Monday he would have breakfast at LaBrinks Restaurant at exactly 7:30. At 7:30 everything had better be on the table or there would be trouble. After breakfast he would go to the office and have a staff meeting at exactly 9:00. Mr. Lucas was so precise, one could set their watch by him. On Friday, he would fly from New York to Seattle in his personal Lear Jet. The jet would leave at exactly 9:05. For one month Louie Sivella, the man who was supposed to eliminate James Lucas, logged everything his target did. The time, the method, the way and the purpose was logged, and finally it was determined what would be used to terminate Mr. Lucas.

"Early Friday morning, Louie went to the airport and pretended to be a mechanic. He said he was going to check out Mr. Lucas' jet before they left for Seattle. He placed a small piece of plastic explosive in the panel of the right engine. He then placed a 10-pound box of plastic explosives in the baggage area. The plane took off right on time and flew for two hours. At 11:05 the pilot radioed the nearest tower and informed them they had just lost the right engine due to a fire. The tower asked if they were declaring an emergency, and the pilot said they could fly with one engine. While the tower was talking to the pilot, the radio went dead and the tower lost the plane on radar.

"The next morning the newspapers called the crash pilot error. The pilot failed to shut off the flow of fuel to the burning engine, and the plane blew up in mid-air. It was the perfect crime. Five men died in order to put the largest credit card company out of business. Also, when Michael and Dr. Messenger said they did not want any traces, what they meant was to kill the person or persons who blew up the plane. When Louie Sivella went to pick up his money, he was shot five times in the head. All traces had been eliminated. Michael and Dr. Messenger were murderers. It would not be the last time they would kill to gain control of the world. Within two years, there would only be two credit card companies in the world for Michael to contend with.

"Michael had almost accomplished what he had set out to do, and that was to have the only credit card company in the world. He also wanted to have the only computer company in the world. In March of 2007, his scheme to put all the other computer companies out of business came to light. With all the games and other software programs he had developed, he decided he must do something drastic. He contacted a modem company and asked if they were interested in selling their company. The owner said it would cost more money than Michael had. Michael asked what the figure was, and he was told $80 million. Michael asked if he wanted it in cash or a check. Michael now owned the largest modem company in the world. He also bought a company that made keyboards. The only remaining company to buy was a monitor company. He inquired about different companies and finally decided on the one he thought was the best buy. Michael had everything he needed to put all computer companies out of business.

"The companies that had been using his computer system were very numerous, but not the size that he wanted. The computer system, software programs, games and other computer-related items would be packaged into one package. Michael would rent his package for $50 a month. Any business or any person could rent his package deal. Everyone would receive a modem, a keyboard, a surge protector and a monitor. When you turned on the surge protector, everything would turn on. Once everything was on, the pass word would have to be typed in, in order to access the main computer at the headquarters. When access was established, the person had at his fingertips everything Michael had developed. The plan started slow, but in time it caught on, and people were renting his package deal instead of paying $2,000 or $3,000 for a new computer system that would be obsolete within six months.

"By the end of 2008, Michael's system was in almost half of the homes in the United States and in three-fourths of the homes in Great Britain. Michael's computer system had taken over as the language of preference for almost all the companies in the world. There were some companies that were not willing to use Michael's system, but it would just be a matter of time until that changed. Michael had given all companies in the world an ultimatum. By the end of 2009, if they had not changed over to his system, they would be totally logged out. Companies were changing over as fast as they could. They knew what the result would be if they did not change. Over 90 percent of all the companies in the world were using Michael's system, and if the remaining companies did not change, they would go bankrupt.

"By the end of 2009, Michael's dream had come true. He had the only computer company in the world. He had put all the other computer companies in the world out of business. He could now manipulate the system the way he wanted. Some people still had old computer systems in their homes, but if they wanted to log onto the Internet or use games or do anything current, they had to rent Michael's system. Many people continued to resist, but it was useless. Almost all transactions were done with the computer, and every company was using Michael's system. It was inevitable if a person was going to use a computer they would have to have Michael's system.

"In 2010, the first price increase occurred since Michael had put his package deal on the market. Instead of paying $50 a month, everyone would be charged $100. With the increase in price, he was also upgrading the modems and monitors. The new modems would send and receive everything six times faster than before. The new monitors were also bigger and better. The monitors were a full 27 inches. Plus Michael's new invention, which made monitors crystal clear, was better than the high resolution monitors they had replaced. One other thing Michael neglected telling anyone about was the camera that was installed in every monitor. The camera had a micro fiber-optic lens the size of pencil lead. This way, Michael could see into every home in the world and keep track of anyone he chose, providing they were in the room with the computer.

"By July of 2010, Michael did away with the passwords and gave everyone an access code in order to get into his main frame computer. His main idea was to keep track of people in case it was ever necessary to do so. Every country had a certain code. The United States would have the code of 555. Great Britain would have the code of 543. By every country having a code, Michael would know where the person was when he was accessing the main frame.

"When a person or company was accessing the main frame, he or she would first type in the country's number. Second, they would have to type in the telephone number they were calling from. Third, they would have to type in a 10-digit code that was assigned from Michael. If a person was calling from Kansas, they would type in the country number 555, the area code for Kansas (913), the telephone number they were calling from (799-9999), and their 10-digit number assigned from Michael (1234567890). The first thing Michael's system did was to check to see if the call was placed from the correct country. If it was not, the system would require the caller to put in the correct country number. If the caller did not put in the correct country number, the system would tell the caller which country they were calling from, and the correct number for that country. The system would then check to see if the area code was correct and if the telephone number was correct. If they were correct, the only thing left to do was to put in your special 10-digit code. If everything checked out correctly, you could then access the main frame. It may seem as if it took forever to access the main frame, but to check all those numbers it only took 1.5 seconds.

"With each system having a camera in the picture tube, Michael's people could see the person who was using the main frame. Many times people would use false country numbers and false area codes to try to access the main frame, but with Michael's system being foolproof, no one was able to break the system. Telephone fraud came to a dead stop. The system was working to fight crime.

"People thought the new system was great when it first came out, but as time went by people were hating the system more and more. The system knew who you were, where you were and what you were doing. If the people had known about the hidden cameras, they would have stopped using Michael's system. Michael had a system main frame in every country in the world. By having a system main frame in every country, the system could check out the numbers quicker and accurately.

"Michael and Dr. Messenger used $200 million to place their own satellites into orbit around the earth. They paid the French government to place 20 satellites around the world. The way the satellites were placed into orbit, any place in the world had instant access to Michael's headquarters. Also, within each satellite, a canister was placed that contained a special type of chemical that would be used in the near future. In the future countries would fear the satellites that Michael had placed in orbit. Even though Michael and Dr. Messenger did not know when the rapture would occur, they knew the time was very close. Within eight months, the trumpet would sound and the Christians would be removed from the face of the earth.

"Michael and Dr. Messenger would do anything to help their program of world control. The Global Stock Exchange was working just the way Michael had hoped it would work. Michael and Dr. Messenger used their friends in New York to place bugs in the offices of every stock exchange in the world. They knew everything that was being said and every plan that was being implemented. There wasn't anything they did not know. They had friends in the newspaper business, and when they heard of company infighting they would tell their friends and it would be front page news. Also, the stock exchanges throughout the world did not know Michael was the writer of the computer system they were using. The only thing the companies knew was the name of the owner, Diabolos. They never put Diabolos with Michael. The only person in the world, besides Dr. Messenger, who knew Michael was Diabolos was me. Michael's goal was to put all stock exchanges out of business by 2010. If he did not have all the stock exchanges out of business by 2010, he had only one plan left to put them out of business. He would inform the stock exchanges they would not be able to rent the computer system to them because of a conflict of interest. The stock exchanges would have to find another computer system to use. Since Michael's computer system was the only one in use by all the companies in the world, the stock exchanges would go bankrupt. And, as Michael put it, 'That's terrible.'

"Before 2010, Michael had put six stock exchanges out of business. The Arab Stock Exchange, located in Cairo, was the first to go out of business. Michael had friends in different stock exchanges to start a rumor that the Arab Stock Exchange was cheating investors out of millions. Michael accessed the computer for the Arab Stock Exchange and put figures in that showed how they were cheating customers. In order to prove they were not cheating, they asked for an international investigation and a check of all their books and records. When the investigation started, there was nothing found that proved they had cheated their customers. One investigator asked if he could get into their computer and see if there was anything there. With officials looking on, the investigator found records of cheating and corruption. Hidden bank accounts, hidden or stolen stocks and bonds and secret Swiss bank account numbers. Everything that was found was proof beyond a shadow of a doubt. The Arab Stock Exchange went out of business within one week of the finding. Michael had planted all the information, and he also had the money put into the bank accounts and into the Swiss accounts also. The hidden stocks and bonds were all part of Michael's plan.

"In July of 2008, there remained only three stock exchanges in the world. Michael was going to do whatever had to be done to put the other two out of business. Michael and Dr. Messenger had talked about different methods they could use on the two remaining companies. One method that had worked before to put another company out of business was to spread rumors about company mergers and companies trying a hostile takeover. Michael decided he wanted something a little more sophisticated than to spread rumors.

"The CEO of the Cambridge Stock Exchange, located in England, was a very young man by CEO standards. He was 42 years old. The plan would be for Michael to write a computer program that would use the image of a person's picture and transpose it to a plastic mold. The plastic mold could then be filled with a thin layer of rubber to make an exact image of the person in the picture. Dr. Messenger asked one of his photographer friends if he could get four or five good pictures of Melvin A. Brooks. The pictures were taken at various functions and given to Dr. Messenger. Michael took the pictures that had been taken of Mr. Brooks and entered them into his program. The mold had a thin layer of rubber placed inside, and a perfect image of Mr. Brooks was the result. After painting and putting hair on the rubber image, it could pass for the CEO of the Cambridge Stock Exchange.

"On Friday night there was a banquet that Mr. Brooks went to. His wife had to stay home with one of their sick children, so he went by himself. At the banquet, someone placed a drug in Mr. Brook's drink that made him nauseated. He left, but had to stop every minute in order to throw up. The 10-minute drive home took two hours. During that two hours, Michael had another man put on the image of Mr. Brooks and go to a hotel where there was a young, beautiful woman. There was a camera inside the room and everything they did was recorded. The next morning, the newspapers showed two pictures of Mr. Brooks inside a hotel with a 23-year-old model. The source of the pictures said they had more pictures and for the right price they would sell them. The pictures were sold to the newspaper, and questions were being asked about the CEO of the Cambridge Stock Exchange. The young woman said she and Melvin had been having an affair for almost six months. She also said she told Melvin she was going to have a baby, and Melvin had agreed to leave his wife for her. When questioned by his wife, he denied everything that had been said. When she watched the video, she was convinced he was cheating and had lied about Friday night. She took the three kids, left the home and filed for divorce. The Board of Directors fired Mr. Brooks and began looking for a replacement when their clients starting leaving and going to the other stock exchanges. The scandal was too much for the exchange. They closed the doors two weeks after the scandal went public.

"When the Cambridge Stock Exchange closed its doors, there was only one stock exchange left to put out of business. That would be the next challenge for Michael.

The handwriting was already on the wall. The remaining stock exchange could not last for long. Within six months, the only stock exchange company in the world was the Global Stock Exchange. The dream Michael shared with the class at the beginning of his second year at Hebrew University came true.

"I have shared with you the things that occurred during those years after Michael graduated. At the end of 2010, everything was set up so the one world government could come into being and the tribulation was less than four months away.

"I will now take a few questions.

"Teresa, what is your question?"

"Everything you have told us about the things Michael wanted to accomplish in a short period of time was accomplished. Is there anything else Michael wanted to accomplish in the time that was left?"

"First, let me remind you that Michael, nor Dr. Messenger, nor anyone in the world knew when the rapture would occur. Michael and Dr. Messenger knew the time was very close; that was the reason they were trying to get everything accomplished as quickly as possible. There were still a number of things Michael knew would have to be finished within a short period of time. The first thing he wanted to do was to perfect the robot that looked exactly like him. He knew the robot might come in handy in the future. The second was to set up branch offices in every country of the world. The third thing he wanted to do was to be president of the Revised Roman Empire, better known as the European Common Market. He remembered the things I had told him about the Common Market and how the world ruler would be the president of the Revised Roman Empire during the tribulation. The last area he wanted was one of the first four things I had suggested he would have to control in order to take over the world. One currency. If there was one currency for the whole world, he could control the world economy."

"Will there be one currency in the world?"

"Yes. During the tribulation the ECU dollar will be the only currency used during the last 3-1/2 years."

"Can you tell more about the robot or the image?"

"Yes. I will be telling you about the robot and the other things I just mentioned in days to come.

"Joshua, do you have a question?"

"You have not said much about Tom and Debbie before the rapture. Why?"

"The reason I have not said much is because there is not much that Tom and Debbie did before the rapture. If you remember, I told you they accepted Christ the day the rapture occurred. What they did after the rapture, I will cover in more detail.

"Let me backtrack and tell you what happened to Tom and Debbie during the last four or five years before the rapture, which made it possible for them to make it through the tribulation."

CHAPTER 9

"**IF YOU REMEMBER,** Michael visited me in Oklahoma in 2002, during our summer vacation. We traveled to Dallas and saw all the sights and later I introduced Michael to Professor Hale and to his parents, Tom and Debbie. Tom and Michael talked and acted as if they had known each other for years. Michael told Tom about some commercials he would be putting together some day in the future and he asked Tom if he would be interested. Michael made him an offer of $250,000 a year. Tom, do you remember what you said to Michael?"

" Yes. I asked, 'When do you want me to start?' Michael said he would call when it was time to do the commercials."

"When I received my two crowns in heaven, I requested that I might have this community because Tom and Debbie were here. Jesus said He knew I wanted to be here, and He had already planned to give me Clearmount. I have talked to Tom, and he said he was willing to tell you about his life the last four or five years before the rapture. At this time I need to return to the New Jerusalem, so Tom will tell you what happened."

"It is just as brother Steven stated; Michael and I hit it off immediately. We talked and shared different things that most young men never even think to talk about. I found that Michael was very interesting to talk to. The knowledge he had on almost any subject I brought up amazed me. He seemed to be a walking encyclopedia.

We sat and talked, and when it was time for him and Steven to leave, I was very sorry we did not have more time together.

"In the fall of 2005 I received a call from Michael. He said the commercials we had discussed were about to become a reality. He asked if I was still interested in making commercials. I told him I was still interested, but because the cost of living had gone up since we last talked, the money might not be enough. Michael paused for a moment and said, 'You sly fox, you are just like me.' We both laughed, and he agreed to give me $300,000 a year. He said the commercials would be made from January through October. The crew would have five months off, and the commercial filming would start again in April. I asked where the commercials were going to be made, and he said all over the world.

"I told Debbie we were going to be celebrities. She asked what I meant. I told her Michael had called and said he wanted us to make commercials for him and I agreed we would do it. We had to have everything ready to go by the last week of December.

"I talked to Charlie and asked if he thought it was a good idea. He said if we did not like it, all we would have to do is catch the next plane home. Michael said the first shooting would take place in Rome. After Rome, we would be in Jerusalem, then Babylon, Brussels, New York, Hong Kong, Tokyo and almost every major city in the world. The idea was to let everyone see the older generation using credit cards instead of money. There really wasn't much to say in the commercials. We had to act excited about having a credit card and excited about using it. That would be easy enough.

"I called Michael and told him I would like to arrive a couple of days early so we could get settled into our apartment, or hotel, or wherever we would be living. Michael said we would be living with him in his mansion.

"On December 29, we arrived at the airport to get our tickets and leave for Rome. We were told to go to gate 37, where we would board the plane. When we arrived at gate 37, there was one man waiting for us. I told him who I was and that we were supposed to board the jet at gate 37. We followed him through the long corridor until we met two women at the door of the jet. They were not stewardesses. Their dresses were not uniforms. Once we were inside, the man closed the door behind us. One of the women said we could sit anywhere we wanted. When we walked into the passenger area, I was speechless! We were the only passengers on board.

"I said, 'You mean you are going to fly a jet to Rome with only two passengers?' She stated that this was the private jet of Michael D. Glispbe and only very, very, important people are allowed this type of treatment.

"After the plane took off, I decided to get a glass of water. While I was getting the water, I overheard the two women asking each other who we were. Neither one knew who we were, but they did a lot of speculating. One said, 'It could be Michael's parents,' but the other said she had heard that his parents were killed in a fire. The other lady said, 'Maybe they are his grandparents.' The other replied that Michael had told her his grandmother would never get on a plane and fly. 'She is deathly afraid of flying.' They talked back and forth and could never come up with anything they both agreed on.

"At that time, I said, 'We are friends of Michael, and we will be making commercials for one of his companies.' They seemed relieved we were not really important people. I think they were afraid we might say something to Michael if we had a bad flight to Rome. Everything went fine, and when we left the plane I told them I would enjoy flying with them again. They both smiled a smile of true pleasure and relief.

"At the airport a man in a chauffeur's uniform met us and said he would take us to Michael's home. The car was a stretch limousine. We discovered that Michael did not do anything in a small way or inexpensively. His home was a 72-room, five-story mansion. Every room was arrayed with the most expensive furniture and decor money could buy. Michael greeted us at the door and said how happy he was that we were there.

"That night we talked until one in the morning. Everything we needed was at our fingertips. If we asked, it was done immediately. When we went out window shopping, if we saw something we thought was nice, Michael had informed our guides to buy it for us. We both had to watch what we said. I remember one day I saw a horse and made the comment it was the most beautiful horse I had ever seen. Before the day was over, the horse was ours. I had to find a place to board the horse. When I made the statement, 'Too bad we don't have a barn for the horse,' the next day a truck pulled up and unloaded a load of wood. Within three days, a barn was built for the horse. The barn was built just before a big snowstorm hit. No one ever rode that horse. Sometimes when I would get a little depressed or lonely, I would go out and talk to him.

"The commercials were put on hold because of the rare winter storm that had hit Italy. It would be at least two weeks before we could start shooting. When we finally started doing commercials, I was a little camera shy. But after three or four commercials, I became an old hand at making them. Debbie seemed to be at ease all the time. She never did sweat or get nervous, like I would do sometimes. We only had a few lines to say. Most of the time the commentator did all the speaking. The people who wrote the commercials really were good at their job. They knew how to make people believe they really did deserve to have the ICAN card and they deserved to use it as often as they needed to. Every commercial had the motto, 'ICAN charge anything I want, because I DESERVE it.' When we first started doing commercials, the elderly, from 60 and up, were using the credit card only 5 percent of the time. Within three months, the percent rose to 17 percent. The commercials were working. More and more elderly people were getting and using the ICAN card. The card did protect them from carrying a lot of cash, and dangerous as the world was getting, with people being robbed in broad daylight, this seemed to be a blessing.

"As I just stated, the winter storm kept us from doing any commercials for almost two weeks. During that time, we were given the script for the next seven commercials. After I memorized them, I could do them in my sleep. Michael asked if I felt comfortable with the scripts, and I told him it would be a piece of cake.

"Throughout the week, Michael and I would have talks at night and discuss all kinds of subjects. He would ask for my advice on many different things, and I would explain why I suggested what I did. Many times Michael would take my advice, and things would work out just fine. One night he asked if I was a Christian. I told him I did not believe all that stuff that Christians talk about and believe in. He said, 'You do not believe Jesus is God?'

"I told him, 'I do not believe a man could ever be God, but some people put men into the position of God.'

"He asked, 'How can you have a son that is a Christian and teaches at a Christian University and not be saved yourself?'

"I explained that some people want to believe anything. They want to believe there is life after death and there must be some way to reach that goal. With Christians, it is Jesus Christ. While other religions have their way to reach that goal, they all want to believe they will be the ones who make it to their type of heaven. I told him I didn't know of any religion that taught their own followers were lost. It is always the other religions that are lost.

"Michael said, 'I can see that we are going to have a great relationship together.'

"The first commercial we did, we wore old torn clothes, with dirt all over our faces. We walked out of an old decrepit house to the mail box. Inside the mail box was a letter with our new ICAN credit cards. The commentator said, 'Without the ICAN credit card, we would continue to live the way we had been living.' We looked at each other with sad, forlorn faces. In the next scene, we appeared with clean and fancy clothes on. We were walking out of our brand new house and saying, 'Without the ICAN credit card, we could never have dreamed it was possible to have all of these luxuries.' The director of the commercial said it was perfect. I thought to myself, 'It sure does pay good to say only one or two lines.'

"One day, in between commercials, Michael received a call from Ireland. He said nothing, but I could tell he was upset. I asked if he wanted to talk about the call. He said he should not let his personal life interfere with me. I told him I was there for him to talk to and to confide in. He said his grandmother, Kim, called to say his grandfather had died. He would be leaving the next day to make arrangements for the funeral. Michael told me the story of his family dying in a fire when he was a small boy. He said his grandfather and grandmother raised him as their own son. That was the main reason he did not believe in God. If there was a God, he would not have taken his family in a fire. Michael also told me how he was ridiculed by the boys in school because he was not Jewish. He said he was one-fourth Jewish, but the other children would not accept that as being Jewish.

"All through school, there were slurs and things said that really did hurt. He said he hated all Jews and one day he would get even. Although I sat and listened to what he was saying, I was wondering why Michael did not make friends outside the Jewish community. When he was through talking, I asked him that question. He said he did have two friends, but his grandmother was a very orthodox Jew, and she forbade him to speak to or have anything to do with Gentiles. It seemed odd that she felt that way, seeing that her husband, Michael's step-grandfather, was a Gentile. He said she also blamed God for the fire that killed her son and grandchildren. Michael's grandmother had never stepped inside a synagogue again.

"From that day on, Michael treated me like I was his grandfather, and I treated him like a grandson. Debbie was always giving him advice from a woman's perspective. That way, Michael could weigh each idea, then decide which would be the most logical.

"We continued to make commercials in nearly all the major cities of the world. Michael did not keep his word about the salary we were supposed to receive. He told me he would pay us $300,000 a year. Instead, we were given $1 million for the 10 months we worked in 2006. He said we did such a great job, he gave everyone a bonus. What a bonus!

"In October we told Michael we did not want to pack

everything up and send it back to Dallas, just to repack it in March for our return trip. I asked if it would be all right if we left everything. Michael thought it was a great idea. He even made the comment, 'That means you'll be coming back.'

"I playfully remarked to him, 'How could you get along without us?'

"He looked at me with tears in his eyes and said, 'I really don't know how I could get along without you two.'

"The last commercial was shot on the 29th, and on the 30th we flew back to Dallas. It had been 10 months since we had seen any of our relatives. We had a lot of catching up to do. We would have Thanksgiving and Christmas at our house. We decided we had traveled enough for one year. Charlie could not believe how much money we had made doing commercials, and when we told him where all we had been, he could not believe his parents had truly become world travelers. We shared half of the money with our children and grandchildren and put the rest in savings.

"Debbie was very good at knitting. When we were in London, one of the tailors was making Michael a suit coat, and Debbie asked for his size. Debbie started knitting Michael a sweater out of cashmere. On December 20, I called to find out where Michael would be the next day. I sent the sweater by overnight mail, and was told it would arrive in Rome around 4 in the afternoon. The note we put in the box said, 'To Michael, someone who is as close as a son to us.' He called as soon as he received the package and thanked us and said he could hardly wait to see us in March.

"During our five-month stay, I had many chances to talk with Charlie. He would ask questions about Michael and Dr. Messenger. I told him we did not see much of

Dr. Messenger because he was spending most of his time in Babylon. He asked if we did any commercials in Babylon, and I said we had done three. I told him, 'Iraq is spending millions of dollars to rebuild the city to the grandeur it was thousands of years ago. Dr. Messenger is building a 20-story complex for his new headquarters.'

"Charlie said, 'So the rumors are true, he is moving to Babylon?'

"I told him, 'They are not rumors. The complex will be ready in two years.'

"Charlie suggested, 'It may be better if you do not do any more commercials.'

" 'At my age,' I asked, 'where could I make a million dollars a year?'

"He said with concern in his voice, 'There is more to life than money, Dad. The Bible says money is the root of all evil.'

"I spoke a little harshly to him, but made myself clear, 'We made a lot of money and we did not use it for evil. In March, we will return to Rome and make commercials until November.'

"Charlie asked with sincerity in his voice, 'What is Michael like to be around?'

"I told him, 'Michael is a very easy person to talk to and to get to know. He did most of his business by phone from the mansion, and when we did commercials, he was always with us. He said, 'If I go with you when you do the commercials, I won't have to make an extra trip to that city later.' We had plenty of time to talk to Michael.

"We returned to Rome for the next seven months.

"When we arrived this time, Michael said he had two cooks who would cook anything that we might want. I told Michael we would cook our own food if that was okay. Debbie cooked all our meals, and to my surprise, Michael started eating all his meals with us. He said the food Debbie cooked was so much better than the meals the hired cooks were fixing, he would rather eat with us. We would talk and just have fun together. He seemed at ease with us, compared to other people who were around him. One day he stated that everyone was always trying to get something out of him, except us. He said we never asked for anything or complained about things, the way the others around him did.

"The year came and went, and before we knew it, we were on Michael's plane heading back to Dallas. The two women whom we had met the first time we flew on Michael's plane had become very friendly, and we would talk to each other on a first-name basis each time. They said the vacation would seem like it only lasted a week and then we would be flying back. Those words became fact. March arrived and soon we were on Michael's plane heading back to Rome. The first couple of months we made commercials in Jerusalem and other Middle East locations. In May, we were going to go to Babylon for two weeks of commercials.

"While in Babylon, we decided to take a tour of the city. The first place the guide took us to was the Hanging Gardens. He stated back in Babylon, in 600 B.C., the Hanging Gardens were one of the Seven Wonders of the World. The cost to reconstruct the Hanging Gardens must be huge. The guide said that Dr. Messenger and an unknown donor by the name of Diabolos had given over $1 billion to rebuild the city of Babylon. He said other donors were giving hundreds of millions of dollars also. With the new religion in Babylon, the tourist industry was bringing in hundreds of millions of dollars that would be used to help rebuild the city. The cost of the Hanging Gardens was said to be $100 million. While we continued our tour, I asked the guide when the government started to rebuild Babylon. He said the industrialization of Babylon occurred overnight. One day there was nothing, the next day there were men and equipment working to restore the city.

"I asked him about the government rebuilding the military after the Gulf War in the early '90s. He said the government did rebuild, but when Michael became the Peace of Prince, all that stopped. The guide said that Michael talked the government into disbanding most of the military and having a peaceful agenda. If they did what he requested, Babylon would become one of the greatest cities in the world, and within years Babylon would become the trade mecca of the world.

"The guide took us all over Babylon. The last sight he took us to was the 20-story building for the World Council of Religious Beliefs. The building was made of marble on the outside. and the inside was a masterpiece of work. It was the most beautiful building I had ever seen. While we were taking our tour, Dr. Messenger came by and asked if we would like to take a personal tour with him. He showed us things in the building that very few people knew about. There were hidden cameras and microphones in almost every room. There were also rooms with beds, just in case anyone would have to stay overnight. Dr. Messenger said that Michael trusts us with his life, and if Michael feels that way, he does also.

"After our commercials in Babylon were finished, we flew back to Rome. Michael had business to take care of, so we did not see him for over a week. I asked if anyone knew where he was, and they said that only Dr. Messenger could get in touch with him. When Michael arrived, I asked, 'How was business?'

"He said, 'Things went just the way I had figured. I

have been working with a man I met in California, back in 2001. He had plans on building a robot that walked, talked and looked just like a man. I bought the plans from the man and told him I was going to make a company that sells robots to the general public.'

"I thought to myself, 'When you have as much money as Michael has, you can play with different ideas and toys.' I would find out later how serious the robot plans would be.

"July 23, 2008, at two in the afternoon, Michael received a call that upset him enough to cause him to cry. He said his grandmother, Kim, had died of a heart attack. He said he loved her more than anyone in the world. 'God has taken another person that I love from me.'

"I told Michael I wished there was something I could do other than say I am sorry. He said he wanted to be alone for the rest of the afternoon. I asked Debbie if she would mind fixing Michael's favorite meal, marinated veal. When he finally decided to come down, I asked if he was hungry, and he said he was starving. When Debbie set the food out, he could not believe she would take so much time in preparing his favorite meal, just to make him feel good. He said, 'I only have two people left in the world that I love, and if God were to take either one of you from me, I don't know what I would do.'

"I told Michael we would go with him to Ireland to help with the funeral and anything else that might come up.

"At the gravesite I noticed the inscription on the head stone. It said, 'My grandmother, Kim, is at peace without God.'

"I thought about that for many days, and one day I asked Michael about the headstone.

"He said, 'The last time I saw my grandmother, she

told me what she wanted on her headstone. She said she did not want any part of God or anything on her headstone that would give God glory. That is what she wanted on her headstone, and that's what she received.' The grief from losing Kim made Michael more and more cold-hearted about the things of God.

"The commercials kept my mind off the things of the world. I was so old, I often wondered how much longer I could last. The year 2008 was almost over, and we would be back in Dallas at the end of October. It seemed like it was just year after year of the same thing. You might say, I was getting a little burned out. The year 2008 came and went, as did 2009. Michael told us in September 2009 we would be doing the last of the commercials next year. I thought, 'How great it will be not doing commercials any more!'

"On March 30, 2010, we arrived back in Jerusalem just in time to see Dr. Messenger leave to go back to Babylon. The new religion was on the verge of taking over the whole world. In two or three years it would be the religion of choice. Michael said he was not that fond of the new religion, but if people needed to believe in something, they might just as well believe in something that they could relate to.

"Before we had left that previous year, Michael said this would probably be our last year for making commercials. There was only one other credit card company remaining and it would be out of business before the end of the year. 'There will be no need to make commercials since the only credit card company in the world will be the ICAN card. If a person does not want to use a credit card, that is fine. They can do without or use cash.' He continued, 'In the near future, the only way to do any type of business will be with the credit card because money will be outlawed.'

"Michael was so busy, we only saw him once or twice a week. When he was in Rome, we had time to talk and discuss different aspects of his businesses. The only company the general public knew that Michael owned was the stock exchange. All the other companies were owned by the person known as Diabolos.

"That first year Michael paid us $1 million for making commercials was the least amount we earned. This year we would make $3 million. What a way to retire. We were looking forward to living in Dallas year round. Well, that did not last for long. Two weeks after we were back in Rome, we were talking to Michael about moving to Dallas for the last years of our lives. He stated that he was expecting us to stay in Rome as consultants.

"I said, 'Since the commercials will be over, we are anticipating a quiet retirement before we die. I am 91 and Debbie is 92 years old. How much time do we have left? Plus, we are not consultants.'

"He said, 'The time that I spend with you gives me the guidance and direction in almost every decision I make. This would be a full-time job that pays $2 million a year, with a three-month vacation.'

"When he told me how many months we would have for a vacation, I knew he really did not have a consultant's job for us. He was lonely and needed someone around him whom he could trust and confide in. I thought how it must be for a person to have as much money as he had and not to have any friends or family. We were the only ones that he called family. A statement he had made one day I hadn't thought about until later. He had said, 'If anything ever happens to you, I don't know what I will do. There is no one that could fill the void in my heart if you were to die.'

"With our age, death was a constant companion. I told Michael when the commercials were over in October, we would go back to Dallas, but we would be back as consultants in April. With that he sounded a sigh of relief.

"As I said earlier, Michael was gone a lot. Most of the time he was at peace meetings between two or more countries. There was not one meeting that he went to that ended in war. Every possible way to bring peace to the warring countries was used.

"In May, he used his computer company to bring peace between France and Spain. It started out as a small misunderstanding, but turned into a quarrel that almost brought both countries to war. Michael put together a peace plan that both countries could live with. The small piece of land that was in dispute would be under French dominion for five years and then Spanish rule for five years. Both countries would have access to his computer company for 10 years at no charge. This plan saved both countries $20 million.

"After Michael would bring peace to the warring countries, the news media always stated, 'The Prince of Peace worked out another plan that brought peace to the area.'

"One day when Michael was home, he asked if he could talk to me about something very serious. He said the reason he wanted us to stay in Rome most of the time was that things were about to turn for the worst. He stated sometime very soon the undesirables that all the religions had been talking about were going to be taken off the face of the earth by aliens. 'When that day comes, it will cause total chaos in the world. But chaos will not last for long. Something will happen that will cause people to think about other things. Also, with the undesirables gone, the world will be able to attain the place it has been reaching for, for hundreds of years. Total peace. The undesirables are the ones that have kept the world in chaos and confusion. It will be a great time in world history, a time of unimaginable peace!' He said he would protect us from anything that may occur. We would have to depend on him for protection.

"The commercial year flew by quickly, and October was almost over. We were excited about going home, but more excited about our new job of the so-called consultants. On our last day in Rome, Michael said he was very distraught about us leaving. He felt the time was very, very close for something to happen. He said he did not know the time or the month or the year, but it was close. 'If there is a great disappearance of people in the world, you need to get back to Rome immediately.'

"The holidays were great; we had a chance to see all of our relatives on both sides of the family. We shared with everyone about our 70th wedding anniversary celebration and distributed invitations to all our relatives at Thanksgiving and Christmas. Everyone was excited about our anniversary, including us.

"I know some of our family members were hoping we would both make it to February 17, 2011. To tell you the truth, I was hoping the same thing also. The time went so quickly, before I knew it, it was February 16, one day before our anniversary. We went all out with everything money could buy. When we were first married, we did not have a lot. The 70th would be different. I spent over $10,000 on food and other things to prepare for that great day. I even bought Debbie a new diamond ring worth $21,000.

"I did not think I would be able to sleep the night before, but at eight I fell asleep and did not wake up until seven the next morning. We were supposed to be at the morning breakfast at eight-thirty and back at the house by ten. At ten, we would have pictures taken of children, grandchildren and great-grandchildren. Then there would be a time of socializing, and at twelve, I had a meal catered in that was fit for a king. I had everything planned. Nothing could go wrong. Well, I might say I did not think anything could go wrong.

"We arrived at the restaurant right on time for breakfast, and at ten we were back at the house. My family and Debbie's family were looking at pictures of our early years and joking about our age. Everyone was having a great time, including Debbie and I. I told her, 'I have really enjoyed the time together and hope it will last another 70 years.' She said that would be nice, but we both knew that was impossible.

"I was getting anxious for twelve to get here so the caterers could serve us the meal of a lifetime. I looked down at my watch and saw it was six minutes after ten; we still had almost two hours to go before lunch.

"Everyone was talking and laughing and then, all of a sudden, there was dead silence. What had happened? Everyone was gone. They just seemed to disappear. Debbie looked at me, and I could see the fear in her eyes. She asked, 'What has happened?'

"I told her I was totally confused. At that time I could hear sirens coming from all over. The sirens were not coming to our house. I could hear women screaming and saying someone had kidnapped their children. Debbie asked, 'Do you think it could be the rapture that Charlie always talked about?'

"I thought about it for a while and tried to remember what Charlie had told me, but I was so confused, my mind was not clear. I asked Debbie if she could remember what Charlie had said about the rapture. She recalled, 'One day, everyone that is called a Christian will disappear.' That was the key! You had to be a Christian.

"I told her not everyone on both sides of our family were Christians. 'Remember Ben, how he used to smoke and use every name in the book when he was mad. That's not what I call a Christian. And what about your great-niece. She has been in almost every bar in Dallas and went home with any guy who asked her to go with him. You call that a Christian? And what about Sammy? He's in prison for murder. Christians are not murderers. Surely he is still there.'

"Debbie looked at me and said, 'Remember, Ben changed. He quit smoking and you never heard a bad word out of his mouth again. Nancy stopped going to bars and started going to church. She said she was sorry for the way she had lived and she said she repented. While in prison, Sammy told the story of an old inmate who was in for life. But he was happy and content. He said the reason was that he had become a Christian while he was in prison. Sammy could not believe anyone could be happy in prison, but that old man was very happy. Sammy asked if the guy could help him, and he led Sammy in a prayer for salvation. Everyone you have mentioned all became Christians.'

"I told her, 'We have to know what has happened.' I thought it was best for us to turn on the TV.

"In the family room, I turned on the TV and the news men were totally confused, just as we were. They told everyone to stay inside their homes and not to leave for any reason. They said there were cars, trucks, trains and planes that were in wrecks or had crashed. Some planes had collided in mid-air, while others crashed on take-off. The reporter said more reports were coming in from all over the world with the same news. Millions of people had just disappeared.

"At ten fifty-two, I told Debbie I thought the rapture had occurred. I did not know if we could become Christians, but it was the only hope we had. We did not know what to do, so I thought it would be best if we were on our knees. I thought back about Charlie and the day he said all I had to do was to ask Christ to come into my life. While on our knees, I told Jesus that we were wrong and that we wanted to be Christians, but I did not know what to do. It seemed as if a light had come on in my head. I could see for the first time what we had to do. I told Jesus that we were sinners and we wanted to accept Him as our Savior. We knew that He died on the cross for our sins and we acknowledged him as our Lord.

"When we stood up, the despair and fear had left both of us. I thought back to what Michael had said before we left Rome. If millions of people disappeared off the face of the earth, he'd told us to get back to Rome as fast as possible. I told Debbie we must try to get to Rome any way possible.

"I called the airports, but all the lines were busy. It could be days before there was some kind of order put back into the world that had been turned upside down. I tried calling Michael in Rome, but the same problem we were having, Rome was having.

"I thought about the things Charlie had said about the rapture and the things that would occur after the rapture. He said 45 days after the rapture, a person the Bible calls the Antichrist will sign a peace treaty with Israel. That will begin the seven years of Tribulation. He told me to mark that date, because 1260 days or 3-1/2 years after that date, the Antichrist would go into the Tribulation Temple and proclaim himself to be God. That day would begin the Great Tribulation. The Great Tribulation would be a time in world history that was so bad that if Jesus did not return, there would be no flesh saved. In other words, mankind would be annihilated off the face of the earth.

"At five in the afternoon, a man came to our house and asked if we were the Hales. I said I was Tom Hale. I thought for sure he was going to tell us some of our relatives had been killed in some of the accidents. Instead, he said he had been sent by Michael Glispbe. We were to go with him to the airport. There was a special jet that would take us to Rome.

"At the airport, a Lear jet was waiting for us to arrive. We boarded the plane and took off for Rome. Once we were in the air, one of the pilots stated that Michael was very concerned about us. The pilot said there would be one stop for fuel and the next stop would be Rome. I asked the pilot if he could tune in to any radio stations. He said, 'You can watch TV if you want.' He pushed a button and down came a screen. The controls were in the chair in front of us.

"The stations were in the same chaos as the whole world. No one knew what had happened. They were reporting on wrecks in which the drivers of cars had just disappeared. One report told of a head-on train collision that totally destroyed a small town when the cars carrying fuel blew up.

"Debbie asked if we were doing the right thing by going to Rome. I told her Michael was a very important person, and if we were going to make it through the tribulation, our best bet would be with Michael. We watched as one report after another told of the disasters all over the world. Suddenly, one report caught my eye. It was reporting that the ECU jet carrying nine of its top 11 officials were killed when it collided in mid-air with a British

Air Bus. It went on to say the founder of the 'Fellowship of Believers' religion, Dr. Mohammed, was on board the jet and was killed, along with all the others. I couldn't believe it. We had met Dr. Mohammed many times when we were in Babylon and now he was dead.

"That meant someone would have to take over his position. There was no doubt in my mind it would be Dr. Messenger. I remembered what he had said as he took us on a personal tour of his headquarters in Babylon. I had told him how beautiful his headquarters were and he must be proud to show off what he had accomplished. He said, 'This is nothing compared to the headquarters I will have in the near future.'

"I asked where that might be.

"He said, 'The Fellowship of Believers' headquarters. I wondered at that time if Dr. Mohammed was going to sell the building. But now, with everything that had just taken place, I could see that Dr. Messenger knew something would happen to Dr. Mohammed.

"When we arrived in Rome, Michael was gone on a very important trip. I inquired about his trip and was told that Michael was in Jerusalem. When the disappearance occurred, Michael made the statement it was the exact time he had been waiting on. Peace in the Middle East was at hand. One person I talked to said Michael was negotiating peace between Israel and the surrounding Arab nations. Michael had stated as soon as the undesirables were removed there would be peace in the world. The peace Michael was negotiating was just the beginning of the greatest time the world would ever know, according to Michael. He would be what everyone had been calling him, 'The Prince of Peace.' "

CHAPTER 10

"**THANK YOU, TOM.** I know the time period Tom covered was very short, but a lot of things happened to prepare Tom and Debbie for the tribulation. Michael had no idea God would be using him to make it possible for Tom and Debbie to make it completely through the tribulation. They would lead multitudes of people to Christ and also make it possible for most of them to make it through the tribulation also.

"When Tom told about the last four or five years of their life before the rapture, he did not let anyone ask any questions. I know many of you have a number of questions you want to ask, so at this time I will take as many questions as you want to ask. We will start with the first question from the front row and take them in order. Tom, if you will take the question and repeat it from the platform so everyone will know what was asked, I will then answer the question."

"The first question is why was Michael so nice to Tom and Debbie? I thought the Antichrist was mean and did not have any friends except the False Prophet, Dr. Messenger."

"What you have said is true. The only friend, if you could call him a friend, was Dr. Messenger. Before the rapture and the tribulation, Michael was just like any other human. He wanted to have friends and people to care about him and love him. His parents loved him, but when they were killed in the fire, that was the first time he felt loneliness. Most people would not blame God for the fire and continue to blame and hate God for everything that occurred in their lives. After a death in the family, the family usually draws closer together. If they do blame God, after a while they understand that God really did not cause the fire. God knew the heart of Michael and how he would react to any accident that occurred. God knew Michael would blame Him.

"There are many times when an accident occurs and the person who is responsible for the death of one or more people cannot cope with the tragedy and blames God. For you see, it was Michael who was responsible for the deaths in his family, and he could not accept it was his fault.

Tony kept all his tools in a metal box and had told Michael, 'Never take anything out of the box.' The night of the fire, Sonny and Mary Beth were sick. Michael did not have anything to do, so he decided to take one of his 'father's toys' out of the box and play with it. The toy he took was a soldering iron.

"He had watched his father plug it into the wall socket and wait for a while, and then he would touch it to some metal and the metal would turn into liquid. Michael plugged the soldering iron into the wall socket just like his father had done, and he waited. After a couple of minutes, Michael touched a piece of metal with the iron but nothing happened. He tried it over and over, but the result was the same. It did not work for him the way it did for his dad. He decided to put it under his bed and find something else to do. He knew he could come back later and play with it whenever he wanted. Under his bed, there was a small, flat piece of metal, and when Michael put the iron under the bed, he dropped it on that piece of metal. When he dropped it, the button turned on.

"Shannon had already called Kim and asked if she would let Michael stay with her because she did not want him to get sick like the other two kids. While Michael was at Kim's house, he thought about the iron under the bed and hoped his father would not look for it until he could get home and put it back in the box.

"The iron was not touching anything that could catch fire, but the metal plate was starting to heat up. After three hours, the metal plate was so hot, it caught the carpet on fire. In less than five minutes, the house was totally engulfed in flames.

"In the back of Michael's mind, he knew he was responsible for the fire, but he had to blame someone other than himself. He did what many others do, he blamed God for the fire. The guilt never left him. Every time he thought about what he had done, he would start to cry.

"The day his grandmother died, he was not crying because she had died. He was crying because he had never told her he was the one responsible for the fire. For all those years, Kim did not want anything to do with God, because she thought God was responsible for the fire. Many, many times Michael was on the verge of telling her he had accidentally started the fire, but he could not accept the guilt he knew she would put on him. He thought she would hate him as she did God.

"When Michael was at the burn unit with all those kids, the guilt came back. He purposed in his mind that if he could develop artificial skin which would take the place of real skin on burn victims, that would relieve him of his guilt. Even after he developed the artificial skin, it did not relieve his guilt. As I said, people want to blame God when God had nothing to do with the thing that happened. Tom, what is the next question?"

"After Debbie and I accepted Christ, why did I call

Michael the 'Prince of Peace,' and when did I know that Michael was the Antichrist?

"I could let Tom answer those two questions, but I will answer them with the knowledge I received when we were given our incorruptible bodies.

"Why did Tom call Michael the 'Prince of Peace'? Tom had just become a Christian and did not know what the Bible said about Christ and His names. One thing Tom did not tell you about which occurred the day of the rapture was before they left to go to Rome, Tom put a Bible, which Charlie had purchased for him, in his suitcase. Within the next 45 days, Tom and Debbie read all the verses Charlie had highlighted in the Bible. Tom would never call Michael the 'Prince of Peace' again.

"When did Tom know that Michael was the Antichrist?

"During the 45-day lull period, Tom read what was about to happen. If Michael was the Antichrist, he would be the one who would sign the peace treaty with Israel, and that would start the tribulation. Tom did not want to believe Michael was the dreaded man of sin, the Antichrist, but if he signed the treaty, that would prove who he was. On April 3, 2011, Michael signed the treaty with Israel and the surrounding Arab nations which was to last for seven years. At that point, Tom knew that Michael was the Antichrist, and with the death of Dr. Mohammed, the only person that could be the False Prophet was Dr. Messenger.

"Tom was in a real predicament. The tribulation had just begun, and he, being a Christian, was living in the same house with the Antichrist and the Antichrist's best friend, the False Prophet. Tom thought about the personal tour Dr. Messenger had taken him on at his headquarters. Each room had hidden cameras and microphones to record anything that went on in the room. Tom wondered if Michael's mansion had hidden cameras and microphones also. He decided he would put it in the hands of God. If he was caught reading the Bible, he did not know what Michael would do. We can say Tom and Debbie were in a real predicament at that point. What is the next question?"

"When the rapture occurred, was Tom or Debbie looking at anyone when they disappeared?"

"Tom, would you and Debbie answer that question?"

"Yes, we will answer that one."

Debbie said, "I was talking to two of my grandsons, and they just disappeared right in front of my eyes, and the people who were standing in the same direction I was facing were gone also. When something like that happens, you are speechless. You can't believe what your eyes just saw, and your mind is totally confused."

Tom said the same thing happened to him. "You have a number of your family members standing right in front of you one second, and the next second they are gone. Even as I tell you, I still do not have words to explain how I felt at that very moment."

"What is the next question?"

"When you first started telling about the things that occurred just before the rapture and during the tribulation, you stated that those of us that accept Christ during this time will receive an incorruptible body. Were you referring to those of us that are in the Thousand Year Reign of Christ, or were you referring to those who accepted just prior to the rapture? I'm really confused."

"This is probably the most important question that will ever be answered about the things I am telling you. I am referring to YOU. During this Thousand Year Reign of Christ, you must make a decision. Will you accept Christ or will you reject Him? No one can make that decision for you. During the next 400 years, I will teach and tell you of that time at the end of the Thousand Years when the Devil is let out of the Bottomless Pit to turn your hearts from Christ. The ones who made it through the tribulation and were allowed to enter the millennium are Christians. They cannot be tempted by the Devil at the end of the millennium. They have been sealed. It is their job and your job to tell the ones who are born during the last 200 years about the Devil and the things that will come to pass. During the last 200 years it will be forbidden for the immortals to teach or say anything about the Devil and how he will tempt the unsaved.

"I know during the last 200 years you will not teach or say much about the Devil or that he will be let out of the Bottomless Pit to tempt people with sin. I know this to be a fact because most of you stopped telling about the tribulation and how Christians gave their lives for their faith in Jesus Christ. If you had told those generations about that terrible time, it would not be necessary for me to tell of the things that happened during that period. Christ said we must teach and tell you who are born during this age, so that history would not repeat itself. But history will repeat itself in much the same way. During the time when the Devil is let loose for a short time, he will lead hundreds of millions into sin and death. That death is spiritual death.

"You have Christ sitting on the throne in Jerusalem and yet some of you will reject. You have seen the miracles he has performed and you have seen that his judgements are holy, but some of you still reject. When Christ walked on earth just prior to his crucifixion, he called those who rejected Him a generation of vipers. They had prophets and books telling about His coming, but they rejected. You have Him on the throne and yet you still reject. You are worst than that generation of vipers.

"Before I take another question I must say there are many of you who have accepted Christ. I am not speaking of you as vipers, but those who have not accepted. You know your hearts, and you know if you believe Christ is the Savior of the world. I will now take another question."

"Can you look into the future and see what is going to happen?"

"The answer to that question is no. The only person who knows the future is God. I know what is going to happen in the future because the Bible teaches it. You can see what is going to happen by reading the Bible also. I am telling you about the Devil that is let out of the Bottomless Pit, because Revelation, chapter 20, verse 7, says it. Read it for yourselves, and also read the next three or four verses. It tells about the Great White Throne Judgment. Those of you who continue to reject Christ during this period of time will stand at the Great White Throne Judgment, and then be cast into Hell, for ever and ever.

"Tom, what is the next question?"

"Jerry, why don't you ask Brother Steven the question?"

"Tom said Dr. Messenger knew that something was going to happen to Dr. Mohammed because of the statement about moving into Dr. Mohammed's headquarters. Did Dr. Messenger really know something was going to happen, or was it just a good guess?"

"What Tom said was true. Dr. Messenger knew something was going to happen to Dr. Mohammed. Michael and Dr. Messenger encouraged Dr. Mohammed to go to Brussels for a conference on the new religion that was sweeping the world. Dr. Messenger was running into a lot of problems with Dr. Mohammed. Dr. Messenger wanted the new religion to be the world religion during the tribulation, which Dr. Messenger knew was very close. Dr. Mohammed set the religion up with the idea of bringing everyone together so they could worship one God, as a whole. Under the religion of the tribulation, there would be no worshiping of God. It would be a worship of man as god. In that type of religion, there were no restrictions on sin or perversion. You did what you wanted to do. Dr. Mohammed totally rejected that point of view. He said everyone must be accountable to God, and with his religion it was possible.

"The idea was to get Dr. Mohammed to the conference in Brussels. His plane would have engine problems, and the only way to get back to Babylon was to fly to London with the ECU officials. At London, he could catch one of the planes that flew to Babylon every two hours. Michael knew the time was very short and he had to become the president of the ECU in order to put together the peace treaty with Israel. If Michael and Dr. Messenger had a bomb placed on board the plane, they could eliminate two problems at one time. They did not know the rapture would occur on the very day they had the bomb placed on board. The bomb went off 30 minutes before the rapture occurred. That did not make any difference. Dr. Messenger had many friends in the news media, and when the rapture occurred, he called his friends and asked about the ECU plane colliding in mid-air with the British Air Bus. That was all he had to say. His friends thought it was confirmed and they reported it that way. With all the chaos all over the world, the report was never investigated. Michael and Dr. Messenger had killed for their own benefit once again. It would not be the last time it would happen.

"What is the next question?"

"In Michael's early school years, the Jewish kids did not accept him because they did not believe he was Jewish, but he was one-fourth. Why did they not accept him?"

"In the eyes of the Jewish belief, his grandmother had defiled herself by marrying a Gentile. However, Omar was not a Gentile, he was Arab. He had been born in Jordan. Omar's relatives visited Kim from time to time to see how Tony was doing. When Kim's mother and father found out that she was not married to a Gentile, but to an Arab, it was worse than being defiled. Kim's mother and father, as well as all of her relatives, did not want anything to do with her or her new husband, Omar, or her half-breed Arab son, Tony. To her family, they were dead. Then when Omar was killed, Kim married a Gentile. In the Jewish community the talk of Kim lasted for years. Even when Tony was married to Shannon, Tony was still an outcast. Tony was half Jewish and half Arab, and he married a full-blooded Irish girl. The Jewish community knew that Tony's sons and daughters would be one-fourth Jewish, and that was acceptable. They also knew they were one-fourth Arab, and that was not acceptable. To make matters worse, their children would be one-half Gentile. Their children would be defiled in the eyes of all the Jews in the community, including the children.

"That is the reason they did not have anything to do with Michael. If one of the Jewish girls talked with Michael or had anything to do with him, it was spread all over the Jewish community. Every girl was told that her family would disown her if she were to date Michael. Kim was so hard-headed, she was not interested in the feelings of Michael, but only wanted to show to the community that her grandson was Jewish and had a right to be there. They never did accept Michael as a Jew.

"However, being part Jewish would help Michael when it came time for the peace talks between Israel and the Arab nations. When the talks first began, the Arabs did not want Michael involved in the talks. They knew he attended a Jewish school all his life and he went to Hebrew University, where he received a degree. They said he would be pro-Israel. Michael put a stop to that thinking almost immediately. He told the Arab delegates at the peace conference that his grandfather was Omar Hassan and that Omar Hassan's father was Kamiel Hassan. Kamiel Hassan was the most decorated soldier in the Jordanian army during the Israeli fight for independence. He became a general and was responsible for Jordan joining the Arabs in the '67 war. Once they were told who Michael's ancestors were, they knew he would be pro-Arab during the peace talks.

"Tom was asked a silly question according to one person, but I said you could ask any questions you wanted, so I will answer that question also. The question was, 'How much money did Michael have?' When the rapture occurred, he was the third richest man in the world. That would not be true for long. When the tribulation began, Michael had control of the economy of world. He would be the richest man in the world in two years."

"You have told us a lot about Michael, but you have told us nearly nothing about Dr. Messenger. Were you going to tell us anything about Dr. Messenger?"

"Tomorrow, I will tell you about the False Prophet, Dr. Messenger."

THE LIFE OF PAUL A. MESSENGER THE FALSE PROPHET

And I beheld another beast coming up out of the earth; and he had two horns like a lamb, and he spoke like a dragon. And he exerciseth all the power of the first beast before him, and causeth the earth and them who dwell on it to worship the first beast, whose deadly wound was healed.

Revelation 13:11, 12

CHAPTER 11

"**IF I HAD** my choice to live in any time period, I think living during the Millennium would be the period I would choose. Every time I come down from the New Jerusalem, I see how nice it is here on earth and I think back how it was before the Millennium. I remember the bad summer storms with hail and lightning and tornados. It was a wonder more people were not killed by nature than the ones that were killed. The heat in the summer and the cold in the winter, with all the ice storms and heavy snow, was enough to make a person scream. But the one thing that bothered me more than anything else was the sin. The last five to 10 years before the rapture, sin was a common companion with people. The Millennium is totally different. The summer storms, hail, lightning, tornados and heat are a thing of the past. The cold winters, blustery winds, ice and heavy snow are just an illusion. The sins that ran rampant before the rapture are not even thought of as far as carrying them out now. Sin does exist, but Christ deals with it immediately. Tom, you remember the terrible storm that first summer I visited Charlie and the remark I made?"

"Oh yes, I remember that storm and the remark. As a matter of fact, I thought about that for years. If that tornado had hit our house and Debbie or I were killed, where would we be? If you and Charlie were right, which you were, I would be in hell, as would Debbie."

"Well, Tom, I think it is about time I tell the life story

of Dr. Messenger, the False Prophet."

"It is nine sharp and everyone knows it is time for me to start teaching. You wanted to know about Dr. Paul Messenger, so this is the day you will learn about the False Prophet. Before I start, I do not want to refer to Dr. Messenger by his full title all the time, so I will just call him Paul. Paul was born in April of 1950, in a small town outside of Midland, Texas. There were not a lot of jobs in that area of Texas, so Paul's family decided to move to southern California.

"In southern California, Paul's father, Jim, did not have any problems finding steady work. He tried a number of jobs, but finally found one where he felt he could remain until he retired.

"There was an advertisement in the newspaper for a janitor to work nights at the Institute for Human Thinking. Having a full-time day job and working five or six hours each night would be difficult, but if the family was to get ahead, Jim had to have an extra job. He decided he would work harder and try to keep the Institute clean, the way he would want his own house. Night after night, he would clean and sweep and wax just to make the Institute look nice for the next morning.

"Dr. Workman noticed how clean everything was each morning and asked who the night custodian was. Dr. Workman talked to Jim and said there would be an opening for a day job if Jim was interested. Jim said he was interested, but he had to work two jobs to make ends meet. Dr. Workman told Jim he would pay him more per hour and give him two hours overtime each day, at double rates, if he would take the day job. Before Jim had a chance to accept, Dr. Workman also told Jim he would be required to take two hours of studies from the Institute each day. After thinking everything over, Jim said he would take the day job.

"After working the day job for two years, the Institute changed its name to Wilson College of Southern California. It was named after the founder of the Institute, Dr. Nathan A. Wilson. After three more years, Jim received a degree from the college. Jim could no longer be the janitor for the school, so he became one of the professors. Dr. Workman talked Jim into getting his master's degree also. Jim decided to take courses from Southern California, and in three years he had his Master's degree. He decided it would be best for the family if he worked for a doctorate. It took another three years of hard work to earn his doctorate, but it was worth it. He now had a Ph.D. in Psychology. His salary increased and the prestige of his accomplishments made him feel important.

"When Jim was a janitor, Paul would ask his father what he did at work, and Jim would make up different stories to tell Paul. Jim did not want Paul to know he was just a janitor. Jim would tell about things he had done at other jobs so it would be interesting. Jim thought Paul would be ashamed of him for being a janitor. When Jim received his degree, everything changed. At night he would tell Paul what he had done at school and tell about some of the silly things the students would do. Paul said he wanted to be just like his father. He wanted to be a teacher. Jim was flattered that his son would feel that way. At home, Jim would teach Paul about the human mind and other areas of human thinking. Jim did not believe in God or anything that had to do with any religion. You might say Jim was one of the first humanists.

"When Paul started junior high school, in 1962, he was not a small boy. At five foot nine inches, he was one of the tallest boys in school. He played basketball, football and baseball. By the time he entered high school, he was already a star. In high school, he lettered in basketball and football his first year and was named to the all-conference team in both sports. He excelled academically and had the highest grade point average in school. In fact, he was considered a genius.

"During his senior year, he was a Little All-American in football and was All-State in baseball. Paul could go to any university in the country; all he had to do was to say where he wanted to go. He decided to go to Harvard. During his first two years at Harvard, he lettered in basketball and football and chose not to play baseball, but his first love was studying. The other young men thought he was a little crazy for studying so much, especially with the drug revolution just starting. The liberal ideas that were being taught at Harvard would leave a lasting impression on Paul for the rest of his life.

"During his junior year at Harvard, many things changed drastically. He had a new group of friends, and their idea of having fun included drugs and drinking. It started out small at first. He tried smoking marijuana but did not like it. He did like drinking, and after getting drunk, he would then smoke marijuana. He became addicted to drinking and smoking marijuana. In the seventies, there were reports that said marijuana was not addictive. More and more young people tried marijuana and found it was very addictive, and in many cases it would lead them into harder drugs. With Paul, it lasted all through his junior year.

"During his summer vacation, he met one of his old friends he had gone to high school with who was deep into human reasoning. That summer, Paul stopped drinking and smoking. He was learning all about humanism. His friend told him the best way to learn more was to ask his father. 'Your father is considered the father of human reasoning in southern California.' Paul was amazed that he had not realized his father's role and was a little embarrassed that he was hearing this from a friend. Paul did exactly that. He talked to his father, began asking questions, and from that day on, his father would teach and train him in the mental thinking of reasoning from a humanistic view point.

"His senior year gave him the chance of a lifetime. Michael started working part-time for one of the largest stock brokers in New York on the weekends. He was supposed to be putting together documentation for a sales strategy for the president of the company. When Paul had a little extra time, he would put together a list of what he thought would be good stocks and bonds to purchase that would make money. One weekend, he left his papers in the office and when the owner came in on Monday, he found what Paul had left. He decided he would watch and see if there was anything to the 'picks' Paul had made. Within 30 days, everything Paul had chosen did exactly what he had expected them to do. They made money. The president talked to Paul the next weekend and asked if he would put together more companies and see if they also made money.

"Week after week, Paul was correct on all 'picks.' When Paul graduated, he was given a job with the firm. Immediately, Paul started making money for customers. During that first year, Paul made the company $57 million. His salary was $100,000. However, at the end of the year, he was the first associate to receive a $1-million bonus. This would not be the first large bonus he would earn. During his next 10 years, he would accumulate a fortune in other areas of business. Paul owned more than 20 businesses with an income of over $30 million a year. During those 10 years in the east, he had time to earn his Master's Degree.

"Paul decided to move back home to southern California. Once he had returned to California, there were two things he wanted to do. He wanted to get his Doctorate, and he wanted to build a new complex for his new business. He planned to build a 10-story building and start a new movement called the World Council of Religious Beliefs. He knew how strong the Christians were in the United States, so he had to give his new movement a Christian orientation.

"First, he would have to come up with a type of Christian statement of faith. Second, he would have to masquerade his new movement into something that it really wasn't. Third, he would have to make those he hired believe his new movement was Christian-oriented. If he could develop all three points, he could be known as the greatest Christian of his day. And if you remember back when I explained to you about the first year I taught at Hebrew University, I stated I could not believe the foremost Christian leader of our day would be teaching here. That was Dr. Paul Messenger.

"The work on his new building began in the summer of 1983 and was finished in 1985. He also received his Doctorate from Southern California that same year. He started to hire a large number of Christians. He stated the new movement would bring all religions together with the idea of evangelizing the world for Christ. The Christians and other individuals who were hired did not know the real intent of his heart.

"Inside the 10-story building, in the basement, he had his publishing company set-up. If he was going to have an organization as large as he was expecting, he knew there would be a lot of material to be published. He began to write a number of books that became best sellers. *The Long Walk Home, The Best Way to Understand People, The Do's and Don'ts in Everyday Life,* and the book that sold over 20 million copies, *The God Within Me.* By having his own publishing company, he made hundreds of millions of dollars. He used a lot of that money to set up more companies, and by the year 2000 he was one of the 10 richest men in the world. He used the publishing company to print material about all the religions in the world. Back in 1995, almost all the material that all the religions were receiving was actually coming from Paul's presses.

"Many times his employees would complain about the material he was printing, but he would say, 'If we can not convert them to Christianity, then we just as well sell them material about their own religion. If I don't sell it to them, someone else will. And that someone else will not be trying to convert them. By having a communication line into those religions, I still have a chance of reaching them for Christ.' Most employees never said a word after that. They could agree with his reasoning. The truth of the matter was he never thought about their souls at all. He was only interested in making money.

"Another way he fooled people was by giving money to Christian causes. He would give money to the needy and sponsor food drives for the poor. He also gave electric fans in the summer and paid for gas or electricity in the winter for the poor. He did what he had to do to fool as many people into believing he was someone that he really was not.

"He also set up his own TV network. It was CCBN, which stood for the 'Christian Coalition Broadcasting Network.' Paul's network focused on Christian themes. It was on the air 24 hours a day. People from all over the world gave donations to the network. Everyone knew who started the network and who owned it, but Paul would never go on TV. He said, 'There are professionals who are paid to do that; I am not a professional.' The network had higher ratings than the three other major networks, seven years in a row.

"To back up just a little, Paul had dated many women during his college days and afterwards. One young lady he dated while he was working in New York was Jennifer Brothers. They dated for two years and were planning on getting married. In the winter months they would go skiing in Vermont. Paul had a cabin built one summer so they could get out of the busy city and have time together. During the summer months they would go canoeing on the lake that was one mile from the cabin. They shared their deepest thoughts and had prepared to do many things once they were married. They talked about having a large family, five or six children or maybe more. During those days, Paul was very easy to get along with. He was never in a hurry, and he was not always thinking of ways to make money. If the money was made, that was fine. If it was not to be made, that was fine also. Once they were married they would move to the Midwest and live. Jennifer grew up in Olathe, Kansas, a small suburb just south of Kansas City. They talked and had decided to get married in the summer of 1976.

"In March, Jennifer starting having problems with headaches. The headaches would get so severe, they would blur her vision. She thought it was too much stress from the job. Paul was already a millionaire and suggested to Jennifer to turn in her resignation. She would not think of anything like that. She wanted to work until it was time for her to have a baby. The headaches continued and increased in intensity until she could not take them any more. She went to her doctor, and he placed her in the hospital immediately to run tests. One test after another came back negative. They were on the verge of giving up until they decided to check one other thing.

"They ran another test, and behind one area of the brain was a small tumor. The area where the tumor was located could not be reached by the doctors, even though surgery was necessary. They decided to take a sample of the tumor through a new technique that had just been developed. A small probe would be place in the brain and a sample of the tissue could be extracted. After the sample was taken, it was analyzed and found to be malignant. Paul and Jennifer did not know what to do or what to say. Paul wanted a second opinion, but it came back just like the first. Both doctors said the headaches would get worse. Her speech would probably be affected, and soon she would most likely go blind. The only thing to do was to keep her as comfortable as possible. They asked how long it would be before she would die. The doctors said she had less than six months. Jennifer did not have six months. She was gone in four.

"Paul changed after that. He had to take his mind off the loss of Jennifer, so he became a workaholic. He worked night and day. The more he worked, the more money he made. He decided to get his Master's Degree while he was still in the Northeast. He met a number of other women, but no one could ever replace Jennifer.

"In 1998, Paul was asked by Dr. Ben David Kent to come to Jerusalem to teach. Paul said he would not make a decision to go at this time because he had a number of things he must finish before coming to Hebrew University to teach. There was an urgent feeling in Paul that said go, but not at this time. He did not know why he had the urge to go to Jerusalem; he just knew he would have to go before long.

"March of 2000, Paul called Dr. Kent and said he would be coming to teach at the beginning of the new school year. He was told the student's year started July 2, and it would be nice if he could be there a couple of days early. On July 1, Paul met all the other teachers and the next day school began.

"That first day of school, Paul met Michael. There was an instant bonding between the two of them. Neither one knew the role they would be playing in world history. As the days went by and the years went by, things seemed to be working in the direction of a one-world dictator. The Devil was manipulating both men to do the things he considered needed to be done in order to prepare the world for complete control.

"Dr. Mohammed was just another pawn the Devil used for his gain. Dr. Mohammed did not realize the religion he set up would be the religion during the tribulation. Paul knew he should be as close to the new religion as possible; that is why he moved his headquarters to Babylon. Everything was set up and waiting for the rapture. Paul did not know about the rapture until Michael told him everything I had shared with him. The last three years before the rapture, Paul would meet with the leaders of different religions and tell them of a time in the near future when a certain group of people would disappear. He made everyone promise not to use his name when they told their followers of the coming disappearance. Each leader promised never to use his name. When the leaders met at their annual conferences, they informed the delegates that one day in the coming future, a large number of people would disappear from the face of the earth. These people were considered undesirables. Most, if not all, of the undesirables were called

Christians.

"When the delegates went back to their places of worship, they told their congregations what was told to them. They said the undesirables are the ones who have turned the world upside down. If it were not for them, the world would be in a state of utopia. They said the undesirables call themselves Christians. And if you look at what Christians believe, there are so many restrictions, they cannot do anything. 'These Christians want to impose their restrictions on the rest of the world. We know we are not alone in this vast universe. One day in the near future we will be visited and our visitors will take the undesirables with them. Then, a new earth which mankind has not seen will begin, an earth where peace reigns supreme.'

"The delegates believed what the leaders said, as did all of their members. Before long the disappearance of the undesirables would be the main topic in all the other religions of the world. As a matter of fact, even the Christians were talking about the rapture. The signs were everywhere. Christ's coming for His church could not be that far off; it was right at the door. Preachers on the radio and on TV were preaching about the soon coming of Christ. They were pleading with people to accept before it would be too late. Many, many people all over the world heard the message and responded with faith in Jesus Christ. I guess you might say it was the final call.

"As the rapture grew closer and closer, Paul was doing more to put Michael in the limelight. After Michael won the Nobel Prize, his popularity grew, but faded in a short period of time. They called him the Boy Wonder. Paul would not allow things like that to hamper his drive to put Michael in the forefront of the public eye. Paul would invent something or would be responsible for doing something and give all the praise to Michael. Sometimes it seemed as if they were working as a team. They really were, but the one calling the shots was really the Devil. Paul and Michael were only puppets for the Devil.

"If you remember the story about my second year in Jerusalem, I told you about a student by the name of Barry Cohen. He said his uncle had found the Ark and I could come over to his uncle's house and see it for myself. When I went to the house, the Ark was in the basement in a large wooden box. When I opened the box, Michael and one other student jumped out and scared me to death. Well, his uncle truly was the leading archaeologist in Israel. Three weeks before the rapture, he and another archaeologist were making digs under the old temple mount when they dug into a secret compartment. Inside the compartment was a small walkway that led to an area that had collapsed. After digging for almost two weeks, the debris was finally cleared, and at the end of the walkway was a door. They opened the door with kid gloves, and inside the room was the Ark. They both knew about the tradition of the Ark. If anyone touched the Ark, they would instantly die. What were they going to do? If they said anything, it might start a war, or worse, some Arab might blow up the passageway. Since they were the only two who did the digging and knew what was in the room, they decided they would talk to one of the high officials in the government.

"Instead of talking to one of the government officials, they talked to an old friend who was a General in the army. It was agreed that early the next morning they would enter the dig area and every five minutes another soldier would enter until there were enough soldiers inside to carry the Ark out. The next day the plan worked to perfection. Within two hours, they had enough soldiers to carry the Ark out and to give protection if need be. A truck was pulled into position, and the Ark was loaded inside along with the archaeologist. They now had to make up a story of how and where they had found the Ark. They did not want the Arabs to be in possession of the Ark, even though it had truly been found in their territory. The next morning they went to a cave five miles outside of Jerusalem and pretended to be digging. Late that afternoon, sirens were blasting, and a convoy of soldiers and trucks pulled up to the cave. As onlookers watched, there was something loaded into one of the trucks. As the convoy left the area, the soldiers were telling all the people, 'The Ark of the Covenant' had been found. The General called on his truck radio and communicated the news back to Jerusalem that the Ark had been found in a cave outside of Jerusalem. News medias all over the world were announcing the Ark had been found.

"Paul told Michael, 'Now is the time for us to travel to Jerusalem. Anyone associated with the Ark will be on the news almost every night.'

When they arrived at Jerusalem, they met Barry Cohen. He said there was a news conference called the next day, and at the news conference they would be introduced as the ones who put up all the money to fund the diggings. What a coincidence. Well, it was just luck, if you want to call it that.

"The same year Michael and Barry graduated, the government had taken away the funding for Barry's uncle to dig. Digging was his life; he knew nothing else. Barry talked Michael into funding the digs his uncle was involved in. Money was nothing to Michael, so he funded the digs for over six years. He always thought it was a waste of money until now. For the next three days, Michael held interviews and said he believed the money he spent to fund the diggings was well worth the cost.

"Paul had been reading about the Ark and what scholars believed about the end times. Since the Ark had been found, they felt the time of the end was very close. He and Michael decided they must speed up their plans in order to have everything ready when the rapture occurred.

"I know there are a number of questions that everyone is wanting to ask, so at this time I will take your questions."

"Did Paul and Michael know what they would be during the tribulation?"

"No, neither one knew they would be the Antichrist or the False Prophet. From what I had told Michael, he knew about the rapture and about the tribulation. He did not realize he would be the Antichrist. He wanted to be the richest man in the world. Because of his desire for wealth, the Devil could manipulate him in the areas that would be useful in the future. Michael would never accept Christ. He had a cold heart toward the things of God. Paul, on the other hand, knew he was destined for greatness. The road his life took would have to lead to something other than retirement and an old folks' home. He knew he would be known all over the world and he knew he would be acclaimed for his accomplishments.

"When Michael shared the things of the rapture and the tribulation with Paul, Paul was wondering what role he would play. Neither he nor Michael knew what role they would play in world history until the rapture. They had a pretty good idea who they were going to be by then. They felt they could win the world.

"When the tribulation began, they knew their roles, and they would play out those roles until the end."

"Is it true if a person were to touch the Ark they would die?"

"Yes, God gave instructions on how the Ark was to be carried. God said, 'Do not touch the Ark; if you do you will die.' If Barry Cohen's uncle had touched the Ark, he would have died. When the troops came to carry the Ark out of the cave, they took long wooden poles inside. Even during this time of the millennium, you cannot touch the Ark."

"If Paul would have been married, would he still have been the False Prophet?"

"Yes, Paul was destined to be the False Prophet. There was nothing that could change what was going to happen to Paul. You may ask the same question about Judas. Is there anything that could have happened to change his life? The answer is no. God does not make people sin, and he does not lead them down a road of destruction. Each man and woman has a choice to make. Their choice is the one that determines where they will spend eternity. Each person has different choices throughout their life. God can look into the future and see each choice they make and see if they have made a choice for eternal life or eternal punishment. Judas, Michael and Paul made their own choices, and they cannot blame God for anything. As a matter of fact, at the Great White Throne Judgment, each person will be shown every opportunity they had to accept Christ. They will also see each time they refused that opportunity. When judgment is given, they have no one to blame but themselves. The same thing holds true for all of you. Some of you are not saved; you have never accepted Christ as your Savior. If you die before the end of the millennium, you will appear at the Great White Throne Judgment. You will be shown each time you had a chance to accept but refused to accept. What is the difference between you and the Antichrist or the False Prophet? There is no difference; all are lost, without faith in Jesus Christ."

CHAPTER 12

"THE LAST two or three years of the 1990s and the first five or six years of the new millennium were very difficult years for the church. Things were changing and the changes were hurting the church. Cults were the fastest growing religions in the world. It seemed they were filling the needs of their new converts. Actually, the cults were leading people down a path of destruction. Almost all the cults taught that man could become God. There was no place called Hell and there was no higher being a person had to answer to. Even the fundamental churches were teaching things that had never been taught before. Preachers were caught in sin, and the sin was announced all over the world. There was corruption, as well as out and out lies from the pulpits in America.

"What was happening?

"Was the church on the verge of collapsing?

"No, the church was not on the verge of collapsing. God was purging the church of the leaven. In other words, those who claimed to be Christians and were not were being removed by the Holy Spirit. The falling away that was predicted in Second Thessalonians 2:3 was about to commence. Second Thessalonians says: 'Let no man deceive you by any means; for that day shall not come, except there come the falling away first, and that man of sin be revealed, the son of perdition.' But it just wasn't the falling away from the truth, it was that people did not want the Bible to direct or guide them in the way they should live. They said, 'We don't want a lot of rules and regulations. The Bible is just another book for those people who think they are holier than thou. The Bible is useless to read.'

"The Christian community was going to face a battle it could not win. In Second Timothy 4:3-4, the Bible says, 'For the time will come when they will not endure sound doctrine but, after their own lusts, shall they heap to themselves teachers, having itching ears; And they shall turn away their ears from the truth, and shall be turned unto fables.'"

"The people that were in churches were going to go after teachers that taught false doctrines. The lie they loved, the truth they would shun. Individuals that were not qualified to be pastors or elders became pastors and elders anyway. In First Timothy 2:12-14, 'But I permit not a woman to teach, nor to usurp authority over the man, but to be in silence. For Adam was first formed, then Eve. And Adam was not deceived, but the woman, being deceived, was in the transgression.' The Bible says a woman is not to usurp authority over a man, but churches did not want to hear what God's Word had to say. They put women into the highest position in the church, that of senior pastor. The churches proclaimed we are living in the modern days, not the dark ages. The sad thing was the members considered it the right thing to do. The Bible had no part in most of the churches that were changing. Many churches that taught there was no Hell, also started teaching that there was no sin. If there is no sin, there was no need for a Savior to cleanse man of sin. If there is no sin, then the church is open to anyone who wants to join. The churches opened their arms to all types of groups. Homosexuals started going to church. When some of the members complained about the homosexual lifestyle, the pastors would say the members were inconsiderate and they should not judge one another. There were many churches that changed and became homosexual churches. The pastor was homosexual, as were the elders. They considered themselves as Christian homosexuals, whatever that meant. Some churches even called themselves Apostolic. What they meant was, they had some members who were elected to be apostles. They did not care what the qualification of an apostle was, even if the Bible gave the qualifications in Acts 1:22. They thought they were apostles, but if you asked their friends whom they worked with, you were given a different story. Churches became festering sores of sin. There was nothing that was sacred. There were contests to see who could bring the most people to church. There were church rallies where you could throw pies in the pastor's or an elder's face. Some churches would even tape an envelope under the pew and once everyone was seated, you could then open the envelope. If you were the lucky person, you won a $50 bill. It became so popular the prize money went up and the church would have to have two or three services.

"The churches stopped being a place where you went to worship God. They now became a place where you socialized. There were many people who had a lot of head knowledge, but when it came to the heart, that was another story. The game was to go to church on Sunday, but live any way you wanted the rest of the week. Many churches even stopped praying. They said it wasn't what the church was supposed to be doing. The job of the church was to get people inside so they could hear the word. Well, the word that was being preached was not THE WORD of the Bible. The pastors were preaching something that was alien to the Word of God. But I am getting a little ahead of myself. It is best if I give you some examples of what I am talking about.

"The Grace Baptist Church was having a contest. The person or couple that brought more new people to church would win a $100 gift certificate to the local Christian Book Store. Bill and Marsha already had eight new people coming to church the next day, but they knew their best friends, Alan and Barbara, had 10 coming. They had to find at least three more people who would come to church. They went shopping at the giant mall that opened only two months before. Just by chance, they thought, 'We could meet an old friend.' They walked around the mall looking at all the nice things to buy, and each person they looked at they thought how nice it would be if they would go to church with them tomorrow. They were not interested in the person's soul, they were only interested in the gift certificate and the prestige of winning.

"They went into one store where Marsha loved to buy clothes. The sales lady asked if she could help? Bill said his wife was interested in a few dresses. The dresses were exactly what Marsha was looking for. While Marsha and the sales lady were talking and looking at the dresses, Bill thought of a way to get one more person in church. Bill asked Marsha if she liked all the dresses and Marsha said she couldn't believe it, but they were all her size and fit perfectly. The total for the six dresses came up to $337. As he looked at the dresses, he said, 'Well, the dresses at the other store were nice also; maybe we should go back there and buy them.'

"The sales lady could see her commission walking out the door. She asked, 'Is there anything I can do or say that will make you buy my dresses?'

"Bill smiled and said, 'Well, I do need a favor and you could help me with that favor.'

"The lady asked, 'What kind of favor do you need?'

"Bill told her about the contest at church and said, 'If you will come to our church tomorrow, I will buy the dresses right now.'

"The sales lady reluctantly asked, 'And where is this church located and what time does it start?'

"Bill paid for the dresses with his ICAN credit card. On the way out of the store, Bill turned around and said, 'If something were to happen and you do not show up tomorrow, I will be back Monday to return the dresses and get my money back.' Before the day was out, Bill and Marsha had talked three more people into coming to church.

"The next morning the church was completely filled. The preacher preached a sermon on 'How Does A Person Get To Heaven?' He started out with the statement, 'The Bible does not say we have to keep a great number of rules or laws in order to get to heaven. We are graded on a scale. Our good works are placed on the right and our bad works are placed on the left. If our good works outweigh the bad works, you are assured of heaven. But if your bad works outweigh your good works, you do not go to a mythical place called Hell, when you die. You just cease to exist. God is a loving God; he does not send people to a place where they would be punished forever. But, the loving God that He is does have a place prepared for those people who are good. That place is called Heaven. I know almost everyone here is going to that place called Heaven. The way I know is by looking around at all the people our members brought to church. This shows the good in each and every one of you.'

"The preacher continued until he was at the end of his sermon, and as the custom was, he would say amen, and that meant he was finished. He did not open the message with a prayer or close with a prayer.

"He then spoke about the contest. Bill and Marsha were beaming from ear to ear. They knew they had won the prize, and any moment the preacher would call their names and they would join him at the podium. Everyone would be looking at them, and the pride could already be seen on their faces. The preacher announced the winners of the contest. It was Alan and Barbara. They knew they had family coming in town to visit and would take them to church but intentionally had not included them in the number they had reported yesterday. Bill and Marsha did not talk to Alan and Barbara for almost two months. Bill and Marsha were very jealous of Alan and Barbara. I said they were best friends previously. Well, it was still true for Alan and Barbara, but for Bill and Marsha; that was a different story. If the contest would have been won by Bill and Marsha, then Alan and Barbara would still be called their best friends. But Bill and Marsha felt humiliated. They had told everyone in church they were going to win. To have their so-called best friends humiliate them in front of the whole church, that was something else. They did not tell Alan or Barbara that they resented them, but they told their children, John and Sammie.

"Both families had a son and a daughter. When Alan Jr. made the high school baseball team, Alan and Barbara were very happy, and they thought their best friends would be happy also. But because John did not make the team, they resented Alan Jr. The resentment even infected John. John and Alan Jr. had done everything together. That all changed. John even tried to pick a fight with Alan Jr. Also, the girls stopped doing things together because of the resentment Bill and Marsha harbored.

"The High Valley Community Church was lagging behind the other churches in the area of attendance, also. They had to come up with a new idea that would get more people into church. One plan after another was suggested, but they were all turned down. When one elder came back to church after his vacation, he told the pastor about his trip to California. He said the church they visited used a technique that brought many new people into church. Before the services started, the elders would tape envelopes under the pews. One envelope had a $100 bill in it, and others had $10 and $20 bills in them. Once everyone was seated in the sanctuary, the pastor would make the announcement, 'You may open the envelopes.' Sometimes there would be a little scream from a child or a woman when they won the $100 bill. If a man won, he never said anything; he just raised the bill over his head and waved it back and forth, gloating. The plan sounded great to the pastor, and it would start Sunday.

"The church put commercials on the radio and also had a small advertisement put on the second page of the newspaper. They said a $100 bill would be given away to a lucky person who was sitting in the right seat. The total amount of money given away would be $300. Everyone had a chance to win. That Sunday, there were twice as many people in church. The pastor thanked everyone for coming, and said, 'Now is the time everyone has been waiting for. Open your envelopes.' The $100 bill was won by a man and, yes, he did the same thing the men did in the other church. He waved the bill above his head so everyone could see the bill and so everyone could see who had won. Everyone was excited about coming to church. The pastor talked to his elders after church and said he had not seen people so excited about church for years. 'The last time I remember people being this excited was when I was preaching out of the Book of Revelation. That was 20 years ago.'

"Well, that is the way it was in the social churches in the last days.

"The social churches did not forget about the young children or the teenagers. They had programs for the kids from the age of two through the age of 18. The teenagers were in the youth group until they were out of high school. The children from two to five were in a thing called the 'Little Church.' There were a number of adults who helped, but the person in charge was one of the associate pastors. He taught the small children all about the Bible from a liberal point of view. He said it really had not rained 40 days and 40 nights. More than likely it was just a local flood. Noah did not really build an ark; it was probably just his weekend boat. He told the kids, 'There was no universal flood, and if there was, how could all the people of the world possibly come from the eight people who survived the flood? Jonah was not swallowed by a whale. The throat of a whale is not large enough to swallow a man.' Story after story, the children were filled with lies. The Bible was not real to them, it was only a book of myths and fairy tales.

"The kids from six to 12 were in a program called the 'Progressive Church.' This program was focused more on memory verses and knowing there were no absolutes. Some of the verses the children had to remember were: John 9:3 — Neither hath this man sinned, nor his parents. John 10:28 — And I give unto them eternal life. John 3:16 — For God so loved the world. These were just a few verses the children in the Progressive Church had to learn. They did not learn the whole verse, just a portion of the verse. The verse in John 9:3, the associate pastor said, 'See? Neither you nor your parents have sinned. The Bible says it. If we sinned we could not have eternal life, but the Bible says we have eternal life. John 10:28 is speaking to all of us. We all have eternal life. If we all have eternal life, then who goes to hell? The reason there is no hell is because God is a loving God. If he were not a loving God, he could not make the statement we find in John 3:16, 'For God so loved the world.' Everything I tell you is the truth, I will read it for you again.' The associate pastor read those verses once again, and he read even more verses to show how holy they were. The children believed they were not sinners and that they had eternal life.

"The youth group was made up of all the teens. They had a great number of things to do. They had dance parties just like the adults. There was one party that was held once a quarter. It was called the 'Booze It Up Party.' The youth pastor thought it was a funny name to call a youth party. He asked the pastor and the elders, and they thought it was funny also. The party really didn't have any alcohol in the drinks; it was fake alcohol. It tasted just like real beer and smelled just like real beer, but it did not have any alcohol in it. The youth pastor never told the youth group it was fake beer. The kids acted and talked like they were drunk. Even the pastor and some of the elders would come to the parties and have a barrel of laughs. What a sad state the social churches were in. The pastors of the social churches gave the people what they wanted. They wanted everything, but not God.

"The preacher taught what the people wanted to hear. He did not preach the Word of God. Almost all the people in the church were lost; they did not know the way of salvation. If the preacher were to preach a message on salvation, that would mean the people would have to change. And that is exactly what they would do, they would change. Change churches!

"Another church two blocks down the street was totally different. It was not one of those churches that had a membership of two or three thousand. It was small, only 82 members. Their church was known all over town as the church of the fundamental outcasts. All the other churches in town had changed, but not the little fundamental church that taught the Word of God. They did not preach the social gospel. The little church was called the Full Gospel Church of Winslow.

"Back in the late '90s and in the early millennium, if a church was called a Full Gospel Church, it usually meant it was a very charismatic church, or one that said all the spiritual gifts are for today. They would speak in tongues without having an interpreter and say it was of God. Or they would have someone come forward that was supposedly crippled and heal him. The people were tired of being fooled and lied to, so they left those churches. If they had used the Bible as their guide and not taken verses out of context, the churches may have survived. They were guided either by their feelings or their pastor, but never the Word of God. They began to go downhill, and by 2005 they were all closed.

"From 2005 until the rapture, if a church was called a Full Gospel Church, it meant they preached the Fundamentals of the Faith, which included the Gospel of Jesus Christ. If you asked the people who were going to the social churches what the Gospel of Jesus Christ was, they would say it was a new hymn. But those who were true Christians knew the Gospel was 'that Christ died for our sins according to the scriptures and was buried and rose again the third day.' Also the Full Gospel Churches preached the great doctrines of the Bible: The Shed Blood of Christ, the Deity of Christ, the Virgin Birth, the Inspiration of Scripture, the Resurrection, and the Trinity.

"The people in the that small church prayed for their members. Also, before the preaching service would begin, the pastor would ask if there were any prayer requests. Every Sunday it took five to seven minutes to write down the requests and then to pray for the sick and the other ones who needed prayer. The preacher prayed before he started to preach his sermon, and at the end of his sermon he would pray. He would give an invitation and tell everyone what they needed to do to be saved. The people in the church were happy when their boys were able to make the baseball team or the football team. And the girls who went out for sports were encouraged by all the members. If any of the girls or boys did not make the team, they were encouraged not to stop, but to try harder next year. Yes, there were rivalries, but friends continued to be friends. They did not hate each other because one was able to accomplish something the other could not. They were not jealous of each other, but they were helping each other to achieve the goals they had set for themselves.

"One Sunday a new family had come to that little church, and after the service they made the comment that the sermon and the songs had a lot of blood in them. That family never returned. They started going to the social church down the street. Not many new people would come to that little church, only the ones who knew there was something wrong at the social churches. When they heard the gospel, they knew they were a sinner and they needed a Savior. They would accept Christ as their Lord and Savior, and that is when they knew they were saved. Almost all of the people in that little church had holes in their jeans, not because they were worn out, but because they were on their knees in prayer.

"One has to remember the changes did not occur overnight. Many years before the churches were infested with non-believers; the seminaries were infested. Professors would be hired, and what they believed was never asked. In the classrooms they would twist the truth just a little. As the years went by, they would twist the truth a little more, until they were teaching lies. Seminary after seminary became liberal schools of thought. It was not uncommon for a seminary to have 10 teachers who believed the Bible and 40 teachers who did not. Some seminaries even had teachers who were members of cults. The young men who were in the liberal seminaries came out of those seminaries very liberal. Churches believed they had to get someone who was 'qualified' to be their pastor. The young liberal men would go into the church, and within five years the church believed exactly what their pastor believed. If you did not like what was being taught, you could leave. The real Christians did leave, as quickly as they could.

"The social churches were doing everything they could to get people in the front door. When the church was not being used on the week days, the leaders decided it was best if they started playing bingo. The bingo games would start at 7 and last until 12. It started out small, but soon they had to turn people away because they were so crowded. Many of the people who started coming on the week nights to play bingo also started coming to church on Sunday. I guess they needed all the luck they could get if they were going to win at bingo. There was one rule in all the churches that were playing bingo on the week nights. No one was allowed to smoke in the church. That really made the leaders of the church feel holy. After bingo started, the church still had one night open; that was Saturday. What could they do on Saturday to draw people? One elder remembered about the tea dances his parents used to go to on Saturday.

" 'We could get a band to come in and charge just enough to cover all our expenses and that might get more people into church on Sunday.' Well, the dances started out just like the bingo, very slow, and soon the social room was full of people dancing. The music that was played was a mixture of just about everything. If the band was really good, they would play a little country, or rock and roll, and they always played one or two tunes from the big band era. Since it was called a 'Tea Dance,' they served tea, along with Cokes, Dr. Pepper and other soft drinks. The church made a rule that made them feel just a little more holy than the no-smoking rule. They said there could be no alcoholic drinks brought into the church during the dance. The social church was getting a little religion with all its rules. But with all the rules, it did not change how they thought about Christ. They made Him less than what He was.

"One pastor said from the pulpit, 'Christ was not born of a virgin. It is totally impossible for that to happen. Christ had the same sin nature that everyone born on this earth has.' The statement that received a standing ovation from the congregation was when he said, 'The Bible is not the inspired Word of God. The only inspired Word of God is what man wants to believe is inspired. Since men wrote the Bible, how can we say it is inspired by the Holy Spirit? If the Holy Spirit inspired men to write the Bible, then why are there so many errors and contradictions?'

"Many, many years before the rapture, there were Godly men teaching the Word in almost every church on Sunday. If you missed church, you could turn on the radio to any Christian station and hear a very good message from God-fearing pastors. The fear of God did not exist just before the rapture. And right after the rapture, people did not have a fear of God either.

"The social churches did what they were supposed to do, they led people astray. They began to die off in 2006. People were not happy with all the things the social churches were doing. If they weren't winning, they felt cheated. They needed a change. But the change would be a real change. A person could go to the little fundamental church, or they could start going to the religion that had been founded by Dr. Mohammed almost 15 years before. His church had an air of God about it, but it was a real change from the social churches. The social churches were not meeting the needs of the members any more.

"At this time I will answer any questions that you have."

"Brother Steven, why would people not want to read the Bible?"

"That is a real good question. In the 1960s, people started to find other things they thought were more exciting than reading the Word of God. They had a form of godliness, but they were not saved. They did read the parts that made them feel good or that did not condemn them of their sin. But sin was part of their life, and to repent and ask for forgiveness was falling from their vocabulary. When they had children, their children did as their parents were doing. They were in the same sin as their parents. They just did not want to have anything to do with God. They just didn't have time for God. I hope that answers your question.

"The next question is: Why didn't the people check to see if the preachers were preaching the Bible?"

"Sometimes it is very difficult to catch a person telling a lie or telling an untruth. The liberal preachers had different ways of saying things that made you think they were teaching the truth. One preacher would hold up the Bible and say, 'This book contains the Word of God.' Well, that is true, but the Bible **is** the Word of God. What the liberal preacher was saying was, if this portion of the Bible does not contain the Word, then I will tear those pages out. It was their call what the Word of God was. And if they say only three or four verses are the Word of God, then their statement about the book containing the Word of God is true."

"My question is about jealousies. Why would parents be jealous of their friend's kids or jealous of their best friends?"

"Many parents wanted their children to be what they never were. They even pushed their children into things the children did not like to do or want to do. When they would see their friend's children excelling in sports or other things, they would get very upset. It is like I said about the last question. Children are like their parents. If the parents like steak, the children will probably like steak. If the parents are jealous of someone, the children will probably be jealous of that person also. It is sad to think people are like that, but the cause was their pride and they were envious of others."

"Why would churches have contests?"

"Some churches were only interested in numbers. If the church down the street had a larger number in attendance, the other church would have to do something to draw more people into their church. The churches did many things to draw people in. One church would have a giant garage sale once every three months. At the garage sale, members would pass out invitations to church, and there were coffee and donuts. If the sale lasted past noon, the church would have sandwiches and drinks for everyone who stopped by. Many people did start going to church because of the garage sales, but they did not go for the Word, they went for the socializing. Other churches used other methods to draw people into their church. One church gave away free pancakes, but the free pancakes were on Sunday morning. By having the free pancakes on Sunday morning, they could get the regular members to church and they could also pull in anyone who was wanting a free meal. Churches in the last days were not interested in the souls of men, they were wanting numbers. Big numbers. The bigger the better."

"Brother Steven, you said women became preachers. Could you tell me how it all started?"

"That is a very good question. It all started one Sunday when Pastor John McWilliams was preaching and he became sick. His wife had typed the sermon for her husband, and she had been the audience when he had rehearsed. The elders helped the pastor to the back, and he stated his wife knew the sermon better than he did, and she could finish it if they wanted her to. His wife finished and it was such a success, she would join him at the podium each Sunday. Pastor McWilliams would preach for a while, and then his wife would preach. When he had his heart attack, she preached for three months. The crowds grew because no one had ever seen a woman preacher. Two years after his heart attack, he had a stroke and died. She became the new pastor. She had authority over all the men in the church, which was a clear contradiction of scripture. If any man in the church said anything about her being pastor, they were asked to leave the church. Other churches saw the large crowds that were coming to see a woman pastor, so they would have women come and preach on Sundays. Similar situations happened across the nation. In the following years women preachers were a mainstay in the churches in the United States. Those women who were pastors and were saved paid dearly at the Judgment Seat of Christ for taking the position that was supposed to be filled by a man."

"You spoke of homosexual churches. Did the people who were members of those churches believe they were saved?"

"Some did, but most were there for the sin. At those churches they could meet people who believed the same way they did. During the week they would meet at different homes and get better acquainted. Those people who did believe they were saved, believed that because they had been told they were born a homosexual. They believed there wasn't anything that could be done for them, even though they wanted to have a life like everyone else. The social churches were teaching there was no sin, and if there is no sin, then being a homosexual was not sinful, which meant they were saved. Some of the lucky ones did attend one of the few Bible Believing churches and heard that they were sinners and the only way of forgiveness was through Jesus Christ. They would accept and leave that lifestyle. But most continued going to the homosexual churches, and they paid with their souls.

"I must be going, but you will have plenty of time to ask more questions tomorrow."

CHAPTER 13

"**FOR THE LAST** couple of weeks we have talked about the things that occurred just before the rapture. At this time I must tell you about the image that Michael created. The Bible tells of an image that will be placed in the tribulation temple. This image will be able to walk and talk and to have a certain way of making decisions. Revelation 13:15-18 says, 'And he hath power to give life unto the image of the beast, that the image of the beast should both speak, and cause that as many as would not worship the image of the beast should be killed. And he causeth all, both small and great, rich and poor, free and enslaved, to receive a mark in their right hand, or in their foreheads, And that no man might buy or sell, except he that had the mark, or the name of the beast, or the number of his name. Here is wisdom. Let him that hath understanding count the number of the beast; for it is the number of a man; and his number is six hundred three-score and six, 666.' Michael had a long way to go before the robot would be able to do all the things that the Bible said it would do.

"Since we are talking about Michael making a robot that looked just like a man, maybe it is best if I tell you where the idea came from. The last 10 or 12 years before the rapture, man was playing with the idea of cloning mankind. Man has always wanted to be God. They have wanted to have people worship them and to hold them up as gods. But the real thing that he has always wanted to do was to prove he is God by creating human life. They said they could create life in the test tube or create life where there was no life. But to create a man that was able to talk, walk and reason has always been a dream.

"In the mid 1990s there were reports that scientists had cloned sheep, mice and other small mammals. Their thought was, if we can clone these small mammals, why can't we clone a man? The world did not want any part of scientists cloning a man, so they imposed restrictions on that type of science. But you know what happened. One scientist said he was going to clone a man anyway. He said he did not care what restrictions his government or any other government set. He really wasn't going to try and clone a man, he just wanted the publicity. The publicity was just what he received. All over the world the news medias were saying how inhumane it would be to clone a man. Overnight, the scientist was known throughout the world.

"Doctors reasoned that if we could clone man, we could take the good organs out of the clone and place them in someone who needed that organ. Just think of the lives we could save. The blind could see, the lame could walk and the sick could be healed. Sound familiar? Yes, it is straight out of the Bible. Can we become God? Or can we become like God? Doctors and scientists were saying we could become like God. All we needed to do was to clone man. The theory on paper seemed to work, but when they started dealing with human life, that would be something else. How could scientists remove the brain or the soul from the human sperm? People read in the papers or heard on TV that doctors and scientists were going to clone man, and they believed what they heard or read. They said these clones would not have a brain and they would not have feelings. Therefore, once the organs that were needed had been removed, they would throw the clone away. The small mammals that were cloned still had a brain and feelings. How could people believe the human clone would not? Sometimes people were really stupid.

"The very same thing happened with abortion. They said the thing inside a woman was not a living being. It was just tissue that had to be removed. The doctors who performed abortions and the women who had abortions had no fear of God. They did not think they would have to appear before God and answer for what they did. If doctors and scientists could clone man in order to remove the organs from that clone, they would have to murder that person. Even a cloned man would have feelings, a brain and a soul. Cloning was not the issue. The issue was that people, who were useless to society according to some, should be done away with and their organs could be used to help others. Who was to determine who should be done away with? Anyone who did not meet someone's perfect 'look'?

"If you remember, Michael met a man in California when he was a student in Jerusalem. The man told him about the plans he had made for a robot that could walk, talk and do anything a normal man could, but he was having trouble with the skin. Michael spent two or three weeks trying to develop artificial skin, but nothing seemed to work. Then there was the big fire in the school at Jerusalem. Overnight, Michael invented artificial skin that was used on the burn victims. Well, many years later Michael bought the plans on the robot from Tim Cabot. After looking at the plans, he knew he had to do a lot of work in order to make the robot look like a man.

"The first thing he did was to use the program he had used to make a plastic mold of Melvin A. Brooks' face. If you remember, Mr. Brooks was the CEO of the Cambridge Stock Exchange. Michael had his picture taken, and the picture was transposed into a plastic mold. A solution was placed in the mold, and the result was a rubber mold of his face. He had 20 molds made so he could experiment with them to get the best result. He let his own hair grow very long, and at what he considered to be the length that was just right, he had it cut. He would save the cut hair until he had the images perfected. He would place his previously cut hair on the images. He did everything to an exact science.

"Every day he would have another idea about the image. He had a speech therapist come in and show him how people pronounce words and the way the lips move to get the prefect result. He wanted to make sure when the robot was finished, no one in the world could tell the difference between the robot and himself.

"The head was the most important part of the robot. The rest of the body was important also, but if you can't fool people with the head, it does not make any difference about the rest of the body. The plans showed the different parts that would be used to make the robot talk. All the parts were purchased and the mouth was able to move, but the mouth must move exactly like the therapist had showed Michael. This was not going to be an easy job. Michael worked on the mouth for months until he had the mouth moving to the sound of the 30 words the program was written for.

"The next idea was to write a program that had a capability of over 10,000 words. Michael was sure he could write the program and he could make the robot move its mouth to fit each word. After two months of working sporadically, he had the robot moving its mouth to any of the 10,000 sounds.

"The next step for Michael was to write a program that would integrate his voice to match the mouth movement. He had the mouth and the words working to perfection. The program he had written would take the word and instantly apply it to the voice. Putting 10,000 words on a disk was time consuming, but it had to be done. Hour after hour Michael would speak a word, until finally he was finished. He tested the program, and everything worked just fine.

"He asked Dr. Messenger to come and see his great work of art. Michael said the robot's head could say just about anything. Dr. Messenger watched and could not believe what he was seeing. It was Michael's voice and Michael's head speaking. Dr. Messenger did not know what to say; he was just amazed at what he was watching. Michael finally asked what he thought about the head? Dr. Messenger said, 'If you could put that head on a body, there is no one in the world that could tell it from the real thing.'

"Michael said, 'The body will be next, but I must have everything perfect before that time comes.'

"Michael had a number of problems that he was going to have to work out. The biggest problem was to respond to speech. If he was going to use this robot to take his place, if the time came, he would have to come up with an idea that would make the robot respond correctly if someone asked it a question. That was going to be a major problem, but he was confident he could solve the problem.

"Other problems he faced were blood vessels, heart beat, eye contact, breathing, balance and, if the robot was cut, it would have to bleed and the blood would have to clot. Problems, problems, problems, so many problems, but he had to work them out. He knew he had to have the robot ready if he ever needed it in a time of crisis. He decided he had to concentrate on the head. The head was the key to world belief. He placed extremely sensitive hearing devices in each ear of the robot. Eye contact would be a real problem, but if the hearing devices were equipped with a directional sensor, the eyes could move to the sound.

"Dr. Messenger knew Michael might be getting tired of working on the robot, so he asked if he would like to take a break and do something that would take his mind off his work. They went to a restaurant and had lunch, and then they just started walking. As they were walking, they saw a new store that had just opened, and they went inside. The store had everything you could imagine. One man was talking about the heat in one of the Arab countries. The salesman said that heat was not a problem.

"The man said, 'It may not be for you, but where I come from, heat is deadly.'

"The clerk stated, 'I have something that will solve the heat problem. I have a suit that will breathe.' The suit had a very, very thin layer of interwoven synthetic webbing. A small canister that came with the suit circulated the air to keep the person cool. The whole suit and the canister weighed only three pounds. The suit was only 1/16 of an inch thick. Michael looked at the suit and asked if it really worked. The salesman said it had been tested to 150 degrees. It had kept the person cool. The more Michael looked at the suit, the more he knew it would work on the robot.

"Michael said, 'Basically, this suit breathes on its own?' The answer was yes. Michael needed something that would breathe so that his artificial skin could work on the robot. One problem was solved, but he still had a lot of other problems that needed a solution.

"They continued to walk around and look at other stores and just mingle with the people. Michael thought about how long it had been since he could just be himself. Being out and not worrying about things and just being free was fun. As Michael and Dr. Messenger walked, Michael started to wonder if everything he needed to solve his problems could be here, in the various stores. He told Dr. Messenger, 'Lets go through every store and look for ideas to solve our robot's problems.'

"One store they went into had a round ball with small fiber optic electric lights protruding out of the ball with different colors. One problem Michael had was blood vessels for the robot. The fiber optic cables could be the answer.

"Another store they visited was a store for Arab clothes. The colors were sensational. They asked how they were able to come up with all the beautiful colors.

"The man said, 'We dye the white clothes into any color that is needed.'

"Michael asked, 'Do you do that here or someplace else?'

" 'We dye all the clothes in the back room.' Michael asked if he could see how it was done and asked if the clerk would show them. In the back room there were 10 large pans that had different colors of dye in them. Michael looked at the red dye and touched it with his finger. The dye looked just like blood. The blood for the robot had been found.

"The more Michael and Dr. Messenger walked around the different stores, the more problems were solved or ideas were thought of that might solve the remaining problems. Michael wanted to get back to the lab as fast as possible so he could try some of the ideas.

"At the one store, he had purchased three suits. At the lab he used the cloth of one suit to wrap around the shell of the head of the robot. He glued it to the head and placed his artificial skin next to the suit. He turned on the air pump and left it until the next morning. If it worked the way he was hoping, one of the biggest problems would be solved.

"The next morning, he checked on the suit and, sure enough, it had worked. The artificial skin had grafted to the suit. He then started to put the hair and eyebrows on the head. Within two days the head was finished.

"Dr. Messenger wanted to come to see the finished product. Michael decided to give the head a real test. The robot head was placed on one table, and right next to the table was another table. Michael had cut a hole in the top of the table and placed his head up through the table. He placed a towel around the neck of the robot and around his neck. He had told Dr. Messenger not to come into the lab for five minutes so he could have everything ready. After five minutes, Dr. Messenger came into the lab. On the tables were the two heads that looked exactly alike. The first head said, "Hello," and the second head said the same thing. On the paper which Michael had given to Dr. Messenger, it said, "Walk to the right and watch my eyes." Dr. Messenger walked to the right and the eyes of both heads moved to follow Dr. Messenger. Next, on the paper, it said, 'Ask me a question.'

"Dr. Messenger asked, 'Is it was raining outside?'

"Both heads said, 'No.' Dr. Messenger walked over to both heads and looked intently at each.

"He said, 'I cannot tell which is the real head.'

"The head on the left said, 'I am the real head.'

"The head on the right said, 'I am the real head.'

"Just then, Michael moved the towel on the left head

and came out from the table. 'You really could not tell which was the real me?'

" 'No!'

"Michael looked at Dr. Messenger and proudly bragged, 'I made a man. I have created man.' They both stood and stared at each other and thought about what was just said.

"Michael said, 'I am a god. I can take the image of anyone in the world and make an exact duplicate. Who on earth can create man, but god? I am god.'

"The work on the robot had started in October of 2007 and had continued for three years off and on. There were so many things Michael was involved in, he could not devote all his time to the robot. In October of 2010, he finished the robot. It was a masterpiece of work. There was nothing like it in the world. He kept records of all the time he put into making the image. If he could spend all his time working on the image, he could make another one in five months if he was working around the clock. If he had a production line, an image could be made in two weeks. The possibility was there if he did not want it to be a secret.

"The things Michael put into the robot were unbelievable. He did use the fiber optic cables, but with a change. One company had invented fiber optic cables that were so thin, they were thinner than hair. He used those thin hair-like cables throughout the robot. In the arms and legs and any place else where there were large blood vessels, the larger cables were used. Michael had invented a special dye that looked like real blood, and with a special chemical in the dye, it would clot like real blood, when it came in contact with the air. Inside the chest of the image, Michael placed a special pump that would pump the dye throughout the robot. All the cables were connected to the pump going out and connected to the pump coming back in. In other words, the dye was circulated throughout the robot just like real blood in a person. If the robot were to get a cut, the dye would clot in the air, and the bleeding would stop. The pump was set to pump 76 pulses per minute. Even though the dye was not pumped throughout the robot that quickly, the idea was to have a pump that sounded and beat like a real heart. The way Michael had the pump manufactured, if for any reason the dye were to be drained from the pump, it would stop pumping and that would prevent it from being damaged. Michael took a stethoscope and put it next to the robot, and he was able to count the beats at 76 per minute.

"Michael had thought of everything. The place where the lungs should be were two large thick balloons that were glued to the nozzle of another pump that pumped air in and out of the balloons. This resembled a person's breathing.

"Michael had taken care of all the problems except one. What would keep the image from falling to the right or to the left as it was walking. Also, if the image were sitting, what would keep it from falling forward or backward, right or left? In the plans Michael had purchased, there were no designs or suggestions for balance. Everything in the plans should and did work. But what Michael wanted was not in the plans. Tim had drawn up the plans for a robot that was made out of metal. The way Michael designed the robot, it was not an ordinary robot. How could Michael's image be designed, or what could be used to keep it from tipping over?

"He called a number of his friends and gave them a fictitious story and asked if they had a solution. One after another could not come up with anything Michael could use. What was he going to do? He had come so far, and to be stopped because he or his friends could not come up with the answer was unthinkable. Suddenly, he had an idea. He connected to his Internet and typed in, 'There is a $10,000 reward if anyone can answer this problem. I have a piece of heavy equipment that continues to tip over, and I need something that will keep it from tipping over.' One idea after another was given, but nothing worked.

"Finally one day, a nuclear scientist sent an answer that might work. He stated that in the internal operations of a nuclear bomb there is an instrument called a nuclear leveler. The leveler keeps the bomb from going off if it is tipped upside down or sideways. The leveler keeps everything leveled just as its name implies. Michael called the scientist and said he had won the $10,000. He told him the money would be sent to him immediately. He asked where a person might buy a leveler for his equipment. The scientist gave him three companies where he could buy the levelers. Michael had one of his employees buy four levelers. He decided it was best to buy four and have three backups just in case. He placed one in the head of the image and connected all the parts together. When everything was ready, he turned on the leveler. As the image walked, the leveler kept it from tipping right or left. If it started to tip forward, the image would put its leg out so it would catch itself. The same was true if it were to tip to the right. The image would move its leg to the right. When the robot was sitting and it started to tip in any direction, the robot would use its arms to catch itself. The leveler worked beyond words. Michael even tried pushing the image over, but the reflexes from the leveler were so quick it was impossible to tip the image in any direction. The image worked with perfection. There were still a few things that had to be worked out, but for the most part the robot worked.

"Next, Michael started working on a way that the robot could have some way of reasoning. He watched some of the old shows on TV about Star Trek. A man-like robot was called Data. He could reason and make decisions. Michael had to come up with a way that his image could reason just like Data, but how?

"Michael could not come up with a way the image could reason. Dr. Messenger asked Michael how the head had given him an answer to the question earlier when he asked? Michael said he had programed the head to repeat what he said to the first question that was asked. The first question had been was it raining outside? The head said, 'No,' after Michael had said no. The problem could not be solved. What was Michael going to do?

"That question was not answered until Michael signed the peace treaty with Israel and the Arab countries. When the tribulation began, Michael had super human intelligence. The problems he had before the rapture were no longer problems during the tribulation. The problem with the image reasoning was no longer in question. Michael knew he was going to use the image during the tribulation, and he now had some of the solution. Michael had a set of eyes made for the image that had fiber optic lenses. He replaced the old eyes with the new eyes and tested them to be sure they worked. The eyes worked just like a camera. He would look into the viewer and see exactly what the image was looking at. Distance was no problem either. Michael tested it to see how far he could go before he lost contact. With his satellite system, he could be almost anywhere in the world and never lose contact with the image. The hearing devices he placed in the ears had to be replaced. The hearing devices were also connected to the master box inside the image. Michael had special antennas made that looked just like hair. The three antennas were attached to the head. If one antenna were to malfunction, the other two were there as back-ups. He also put a speaker in the throat of the image. This way he could speak into the microphone, and he could answer any question that was asked.

"During the first year of the tribulation, Michael used the image many times when he did not want to go to a meeting. He had a large monitor put in his private room in Jerusalem so he could watch what was happening. Michael thought it was a great idea. He could be in two places at the same time. Also, the death threats that were coming in almost every month were taken very seriously. When a death threat would come in, Michael would use the image to take his place. But there never were any acts of violence the first year of the tribulation, there were only threats.

"The first time Michael really tested the image in public was during the first year of the tribulation. He asked Dr. Messenger if he would go with the image for a walk around town. Dr. Messenger did not think it was a very good idea, but Michael said, 'We know that we can be almost anywhere in the world and not lose contact with the image, but we must see how he can maneuver in public.' Dr. Messenger and the image started to walk down the street. When one person stepped in front of the robot, Michael said, 'Excuse me.' The person acknowledged the image, and things worked fine so far.

"Michael had told Dr. Messenger to go to the market area where there were multitudes of people. The image had no problems going through the crowded market place. The fiber optic cameras were working perfectly, as was the speaker. Michael asked one person if they knew where a certain restaurant was located. The person gave the image directions and even pointed which way to go. There were a number of times when people in the marketplace bumped into the image, and each time the image corrected itself with a step here or a step there. Michael could not believe how well the image was working. As a matter of fact, he was working better than Michael had ever dreamed. All through the walk, Dr. Messenger continued to talk to the image. Michael heard everything that was said loud and clear. Michael had thought of everything. He left no stone unturned. Every aspect of the image was covered, nothing could go wrong.

"Michael tested the image many more times in public. One test he performed was his greatest proof. He told Dr. Messenger he was going to a meeting and he would be back in an hour. He asked if Dr. Messenger would pick him up at the house so they could cover some important material with the Prime Minister of Israel. Dr. Messenger picked Michael up at the house and headed for the Prime Minister's house. On the way, Michael and Dr. Messenger talked back and forth, and Michael asked many questions. Dr. Messenger made the comment that he was acting a little different with all the questions. Michael made the comment he was just curious. They met with the Prime Minister for two hours, and on the way home they discussed the things they had pointed out to the Prime Minister. When they went inside the house, they headed straight for Michael's private room. Michael had his big chair turned away from the door. Once inside, Dr. Messenger closed the door and locked it. As they both walked toward the desk, Michael swirled in the chair. Dr. Messenger nearly had a heart attack. He jumped, and then he knew he had been taken. Dr. Messenger made the excuse he knew it was the image all the time. Michael looked at Dr. Messenger and said, 'The image is so perfect it even fooled you. You did not know I was here and the robot was with you. The robot has passed the ultimate test. If we ever run into a situation where we have to use the image, he will be a perfect substitute.'

"Michael did not know how soon he would have to use the robot to protect his life, but he knew sooner or later he would use the robot.

"I know there are a lot of questions that everyone wants to ask, so go ahead and ask. Amy, I know you have wanted to ask me a question, so what is it?"

"You said Michael had the head and worked on it first; I don't understand what you mean."

"When he bought the plans for the robot, he had to put the head together first. He bought all the parts and started putting them together, and when he was finished he had the shell of a head. If he could not make the head talk and act like a real man, there was no reason to invest any money on the rest of the body. Once he had the head put together, he then cut parts of the breathing suit up and put it around the head. He placed the mold of his head on the suit. The next step was to put everything else on the head, such as hair, eyes, a nose, the ears and everything else so it would look like a man. Remember, all Michael started with were the plans. He had to complete everything else from scratch. The speech was very difficult, but Michael was able to get by that problem also. After perfecting the image to his exact likeness, he decided he would test the head. If you remember, Dr. Messenger came into the room and saw two heads on different tables, they both looked just like Michael. One was the image, the other was Michael. After another year of work on the image, the result was a robot that was identical to Michael. No one could tell the difference between the two. Jamie you have a question?"

"Yes, I know you said Michael made the robot to look like a man and to talk, walk and to be just like a real man, but was he able to fool people when the tribulation started?"

"Not only was Michael able to fool people, but he used the robot almost all of the time when he did not want to get into crowded areas. He knew there were people who wanted to be in the limelight, and if they were to kill him, they would be known world-wide overnight. When the tribulation started, many great inventions were used on the robot. One invention was a computer chip that made it possible for the robot to have a sense of reasoning. There were hundreds of thousands of responses to certain questions the robot could use. Michael always wore a special hearing aid. The hearing aid was actually a transmitter. The receivers were in the ears of the robot. If someone said something, Michael could hear what was said. And by having a microphone, Michael could speak for the robot. People in the tribulation never could tell the difference between Michael and the robot. Chip, what is your question?"

"You said Michael invented something that looked like blood and it clotted like blood. Did the robot ever get cut or receive a wound that made him bleed?"

"Yes. On one particular day, Michael was touring the building of the new rail system when he was cut on the arm. Oh, did I say Michael? I meant the image was touring the new rail system. The cut was a very deep cut. The dye was flowing out of his arm, but within 30 seconds the dye started to clot. Everyone was concerned about Michael (actually the robot). That was the first real big test for the dye. It worked perfectly. Who has the next question?"

"Since Michael made an image of himself, why did he not make an image of Dr. Messenger?"

"Dr. Messenger was supposed to be a man of God. There were not that many people during the tribulation who wanted to kill Dr. Messenger. But during the last 3-1/2 years of the tribulation, many people attempted to kill Michael. There were constant death threats and different methods used to try to assassinate Michael. God would not let any attempt succeed. Jesus would take care of the Antichrist and the False Prophet when he returned at the end of the tribulation. Michael thought about making an image for Dr. Messenger, but there were more important things to do than to make an image of one who had no threats against him. I will take one last question before I have to leave. Ed, you have a question?"

"There must be some other reason why Michael made the robot other than to take his place when he did not want to be in large crowds. What was the real reason Michael made the robot?"

"The main reason Michael made the robot was to fulfill prophecy. In Revelation, chapter 13, it speaks about the image of the Antichrist that will receive a head wound. The wound will be healed and the whole world will follow after the Antichrist. I had told Michael about the image and the head wound and that the wound would be healed. Michael knew he had to build something that would look just like him. When he met Tim Cabot and Tim told him of his invention, Michael knew he had to buy the plans at any cost. The robot had to be built and operational before the tribulation started. He knew he would have to use the robot in the tribulation. He also knew if he did not use the robot almost all the time, just before the mid-point of the tribulation, he could be the one who would receive the head wound. Michael knew he was not God and he knew if he was to receive a head wound like the one the Bible speaks of, it would probably kill him. He could not take any chances; the robot had to take his place every day. If there were any attempts on his life, it would be the image that would be sacrificed."

"Brother Steven, could I ask one more question before you leave?"

"Okay, what is the question?"

"You said, 'if there were any attempts on his life' and you said 'the Bible tells about the Antichrist receiving a head wound.' Are you telling us that the robot received the head wound and not Michael?"

"I was not wanting to tell you the story of the incident that would have cost Michael's life if the robot had not taken his place yet. What I will tell you is that there was a group of men who were determined to assassinate Michael. Their plan was foolproof; nothing could go wrong. The only thing they did not know about was the robot. If these men had lived during the times of Christ, they would have been called zealots. But because they were living in a different time period, they were called radicals. Those who were called radicals would do anything to accomplish their goals, even if it meant murder. The Bible says he that lives by the sword will die by the sword. These men met their end the same way they lived, in violence. Later on I will tell about the tribulation and what happened when the robot received the head wound. There is so much I want to tell you, but we must take it one day at a time. I don't want to get in a hurry and leave some of the most important things out of our discussion. Everything must be covered so you will understand how terrible the tribulation was."

CHAPTER 14

"**AT THIS TIME** I will not allow any questions to be asked. This subject matter is so important I would like to spend the whole day telling you about the rapture. This day is the day all Christians have looked forward to seeing and experiencing. The Bible gives two scriptures that tell about the rapture. The first is First Corinthians 15:51-53. It says, 'Behold, I show you a mystery: We shall not all sleep, but we shall all be changed, In a moment, in the twinkling of an eye, at the last trump; for the trumpet shall sound, and the dead shall be raised incorruptible, and we shall be changed. For this corruptible must put on incorruption, and this mortal must put on immortality.' This verse speaks of a time during the Church Age, when all Christians alive would hear the trumpet sound and would be changed in the twinkling of an eye. Those of us who were raptured never experienced death.

"The second verse is First Thessalonians 4:15-17 and it says, 'For this we say unto you by the word of the Lord, that we who are alive and remain unto the coming of the Lord shall not precede them who are asleep. For the Lord himself shall descend from heaven with a shout, with the voice of the archangel, and with the trump of God; and the dead in Christ shall rise first; Then we who are alive and remain shall be caught up together with them in the clouds, to meet the Lord in the air; and so shall we ever be with the Lord.'

"This verse is a very strong verse telling us what

would happen at the rapture. The dead in Christ or those who had already died starting the Day of Pentecost would go up first, then we that were alive would be caught up or raptured. These two verses are among the verses we called the Blessed Hope.

"As I have told you before, on Thursday, February 17, 2011, at 10:07 in the morning, the trumpet sounded and hundreds of millions of Christians were caught up in the air to meet the Lord. You already know what I was doing at that time, and Tom spoke of what he was doing when the rapture occurred. But there were so many other things that happened on that day, I thought it best to take the time and tell you.

"When the rapture occurred, people were going about their daily business just as usual. There was no warning and there were no signs that would indicate this was that promised day. Most people in the world knew something was going to happen soon. The threat of a world war had been on the horizon for years. The threat from third world countries that had developed or bought nuclear bombs was a threat the major powers did not take lightly. The Christians knew what was about to happen, but to know the exact date or time of the rapture was only known to God.

"Michael had put all credit card companies out of business, and also the Global Stock Exchange was the only stock exchange in the world. The computer company he owned was changing every day. Reports coming from his headquarters told of a major change that would take place just any day. No one knew what that change would be, but the last change he made cost the public. He went from $50 a month rental for the monitor, keyboard, modem and surge protector, to $100 a month.

"Rumors had circulated that Dr. Messenger and

Michael wanted an area code that would be unique to their access code. Their computers searched and found the only area code that was not in use was 666. If they put 666 in as the first three digits of the access code, they knew the Christian community around the world would not accept that number and they might even sway the rest of the world into rejecting the number also. If you remember, I told you the computer system that Michael was renting all over the world had an access code you had to type in, in order to gain access to the main computer. You would type in your country number, then the three-digit area code, the telephone number, and last you had to impute a special ten-digit code that was assigned to you from Michael.

"Under the new system, you would have to type in the special three-digit area code, 666. The rest of your access code would not change. Michael and Dr. Messenger knew the time was very, very close for something to happen, but they did not know the time of the rapture either, nor did they really understand what would happen at that time except that the Christians seemed to believe they would be gone.

"As soon as the rapture occurred, the new code took effect. If you think about it, the world had to use 666 for the next 3-1/2 years to access Michael's computer system. When Michael went into the temple 3-1/2 years later, proclaimed himself to be God, and required everyone to take his number, 666, the people probably didn't even think about what they were doing, because they had been using the number for such a long time. Also, with the Christians gone, no one would protest. That was the plan that Michael and Dr. Messenger were banking on.

"A perfect example of what Michael was doing is the bullfrog. You put a bullfrog into hot water, he jumps out immediately. But if you put him into cold water and turn the heat up very slowly, he will cook and never realize what has happened to him. People are the same way. Give them a little at a time and they won't realize what is actually happening to them.

"Of course, for many places around the world, the rapture occurred at night. When 10:07a.m. CST came, total chaos erupted around the world.

"As I said earlier, looking at it from the viewpoint in the United States, people were going about their daily routines. The offices were filled with workers, which meant the highways did not have a lot of people on them. Most airplanes were already in the air flying to their destinations. The time the Lord picked for the rapture was a time that meant the least amount of people would be involved in accidents.

"However, the United States was hit extremely hard, because Christians were located in key positions in the government. Also, Christians were the CEO's of major companies and even small companies. The news media did not know what to do or to say. Dr. Messenger called many of his media friends and reminded them what the other religions had been saying for the last three or four years. 'One day, in the coming future, those that are known as the undesirables will be taken off the face of the earth. It is just a matter of time before it happens.'

"Before the day was out, the news medias all over the world were telling the story of an invasion from outer space. 'Hundreds of millions of people all over the world have been taken. Where they were taken is not known at this time, but we must prepare in case the invaders come back for some reason.' The world wanted answers, but no one had any.

"When interviewed by the media, people were asking, 'Why isn't there someone in the world who can lead us out of all of these problems? What we need is someone to be the president of the world.'

"Five days before the rapture, Michael and Dr. Messenger were in Jerusalem talking about the money they had used to fund the digging that discovered the Ark. For three days, they had interviews and news conferences. All of that stopped two days before the rapture. The Arab confederacy met secretly right after the Ark was located and discussed what would happen now. They knew all the stories from the Old Testament, how the Jews would win wars as long as the Ark was in their possession. Would Israel now go to war with the Arab countries around her? But the biggest problem the Arabs faced was the reliability of the Bible. The Bible tells about the Jews being the chosen people of God. It also says if you are against God's people, He will be against you. If the Bible was true, that meant the Koran was wrong. The Arabs had been believing in a false religion. And if a false religion, then those who had died in the wars with Israel had not gone to heaven as taught by the Koran. The Arab confederacy was in a real dilemma. What could they do? It was decided the best thing to do was to mount a surprise attack on Israel. If each Arab nation parachuted thousands of troops into Jerusalem, they could capture the Ark and bring Israel to her knees. The plans were set into motion and the attack would occur on Saturday, February 19, at 6:00 in the morning.

"There were some in the Arab confederacy who knew war would not help the Arabs or Israel. One of the Arab Generals in the Saudi Arabian army called Michael and told him of the plans to attack Israel. As I said, two days before the rapture the news interviews and conferences had stopped. Michael talked to Dr. Messenger and said he was going to call all the countries involved and ask for an emergency meeting in Syria. The countries that had made plans to attack Israel were members of his Brotherhood of Common Beliefs. The Arab countries agreed to meet in Syria and discuss what plans Michael could come up with to prevent war. Michael talked to the officials in Israel, and they said they would not put the Ark on display to the general public if something could be worked out.

"Michael and Dr. Messenger met and thought about what must be done. They had already set into motion the elimination of the top ECU officials and Dr. Mohammed. The plane would be blown up on Thursday morning, and the attack on Israel was planned for Saturday at 6:00 in the morning. There was not enough time for Michael to be chosen as the new president of the ECU. Michael had to come up with a plan that would work to prevent World War Three. But he did not have a plan to present to the Arab confederacy. He called the Prime Minister and asked if he had any ideas that would prevent war. The Prime Minister said there was only one thing that would stop the pending war. The Israeli Prime Minister told Michael if the Arabs attacked Israel, they would retaliate with nuclear weapons. 'When you meet with the Arabs, ask for a 30- or 60-day cooling-off period so both sides can get together and talk.' It seemed like a good idea to Michael. If the Arabs knew that Israel would use nuclear weapons, they may not attack.

"Michael met with the officials of the Arab confederacy and discussed different ideas, but everything Michael brought up was rejected by the Arabs. They said they were not interested in anything Israel might say or do. There was going to be war and that was final. Since Michael could not talk them into a peaceful means to solve the problem, he used his ace in the hole. He informed them that the Israeli Secret Service knew all about the secret meetings and what they planned to do. 'Israel says as soon as the planes take off with paratroopers to invade, they will launch their missiles with nuclear weapons aimed for every major city in Arab countries. They say they have 120 nuclear bombs and they will launch them all if they are invaded.' Michael said Israel wanted to have a 30- or 60-day cooling-off period where both sides could come together and talk. The officials asked Michael if he would go outside while they talked things over. Within 10 minutes, they called him back inside and said they agreed the best thing to do was to take a 30- to 60-day cooling-off period. Michael said he would go back and tell the Prime Minister what had been decided. He warned them not to try to lie and then attack; Israel would know exactly what they were doing and planning.

"When Michael came back to Jerusalem on Wednesday, he met with the Prime Minister and said the Arab confederacy had agreed to take the 30 to 60 days and cool off. The news media had been informed by Dr. Messenger about the likelihood of World War Three starting in the Middle East. Newspapers everywhere had the headlines, 'World War Three?' They told how Michael had traveled to Syria and spoke with the delegates from the Arab Confederacy and worked out a plan that would prevent war for at least 30 or 60 days. The newspapers said, 'The Prince of Peace has brought peace to the world once again.'

"Neither Michael nor Dr. Messenger had any idea that everything was being prepared by God for the tribulation. They both were looking forward to Thursday. If they had only known what was going to happen, they both would have been amazed.

"Dr. Messenger was at Michael's house in Jerusalem when the rapture occurred. They were waiting for a call telling them of the ECU plane blowing up. They had no idea the telephone call they were receiving at ten minutes after ten would be a call telling them that hundreds of millions of people had just disappeared. The reporter who called wanted to know what they thought and what they were going to do to answer the questions that were going to be asked all over the world.

"The acting President of the United States had the sirens sounding all over the country. People were frantic; they had loved ones missing and they were scared. Every child in the world who did not understand or was too young to understand how to accept Christ was gone. Almost all of the children who were left were 13 years or older.

"In some cities there were riots. Since the owners of stores and other kinds of businesses were gone, it meant all was free for the taking. The police did nothing. They were busy with car wrecks and other accidents that involved deaths. There were acts of bravery also. All over the world people were helping in the rescue of others. In Spain, one man saved the lives of five women when they were trapped inside a burning house. He was able to break down the door and bring the women out.

"Most people turned on the TV and watched as one reporter after another would try to explain what had happened. One reporter was cut off the air when he stated he believed the promise all Christians had been looking forward to had occurred, that being the rapture. The other reporters on that station said it was not the rapture; it was the taking of the undesirables. They would use illustrations of different people who were still left to prove the rapture had not occurred. They explained the rapture as the taking of the bad compared to the taking of the good. 'Those who are gone were the bad and almost all who are left are the good.'

"Even though there were many people missing, it did not stop the sin in the world. Sin increased. There were no restraints. People could do whatever they wanted to do, and they did just that. Women and men who had dreams of sin in the work place did exactly what they had dreamed about doing. People who enjoyed stealing increased their stealing. Whatever a person thought, they did.

"The Bible says when the rapture occurs the restraining force will be lifted off the face of the earth. The restraining force was the Holy Spirit. The Christians had the Holy Spirit dwelling within them, and when the rapture occurred the restrainer was removed with the Christians. Also, Second Thessalonians 2:6-8 makes it perfectly clear the Holy Spirit was that power which was restraining sin. It states, 'And now ye know what restraineth that he might be revealed in his time. For the mystery of iniquity doth already work; only he who now hindereth will continue to hinder until he be taken out of the way. And then shall that wicked one be revealed, whom the Lord shall consume with the spirit of his mouth, and shall destroy with the brightness of his coming.' Michael, The Antichrist could now be revealed to the world, for He, the restrainer, the Holy Spirit, had been taken out of the way.

"For the next 45 days the world still did not know that Michael was the feared Antichrist. However, when he signed the peace treaty with Israel, the world should have known who he was, but nearly all did not.

"The full impact of the world being turned upside down did not hit home until the newspapers came out at five o'clock. The headlines read, "MILLIONS MISSING!" It then started telling of all the people who were killed in car, bus, train and truck wrecks in the country. It told about planes that had crashed and people who were so frightened they committed suicide. Grown men were crying like babies because their wives were missing or their children were gone. Every government asked for their citizens to stay off the streets for the next couple of nights for their own protection, or until some kind of order could be restored. Also, the next morning, on most front pages, the continued story of a possible war was printed.

"The war was taking a back seat to the rapture. Dr. Messenger decided something had to be done to get everyone's mind off the disappearance of millions. He called his media friends once again and told them he just had a call from a friend who had given him some startling facts. The facts proved beyond a shadow of a doubt that the undesirables were the ones who were responsible for all the wars that had been fought in the world for the last 150 years. The facts that Dr. Messenger was talking about were all fabricated in his mind. Since everything used computers, it was not difficult to change the facts to prove what Dr. Messenger was saying was true.

"The following morning, front pages of most newspapers included stories of the past wars that had been started by the undesirables. People were encouraged to check out the facts in their computers. World War One was started when Archduke Francis Ferdinand of Austria-Hungary was assassinated on June 28, 1914. The truth was that the assassin, Gavrilo Princip, belonged to a group of Serbian terrorists. The Serbians and the Austria-Hungarys were not friends and most countries in Europe were expecting war to break out any time. The assassination was the excuse Austria-Hungary used that started World War One. Austria-Hungary gave the Serbian government 48 hours to respond to an ultimatum. When the Serbian government did not respond on that date, the Austria-Hungary government declared war. Within one week all of Europe was at war.

"The information altered in the computer, to show the undesirables or Christians were responsible for World War One, was that Gavrilo Princip had Christian friends and they had influenced him into assassinating the Archduke. The terrorist group he belonged to was made up of mostly Christians. No one questioned the facts; they just took them as being the truth.

"World War Two began in Europe when Adolf Hitler gave the order to invade Poland on September 1, 1939. Two days later England and France declared war on Germany. The story of how Hitler grew up and the Christian friends he had was all a lie. The story placed in the computer said his friends told him he had to conquer those countries that were closest to him if he was going to win a war.

"The public believed what the computers said, so they also believed the story of the attack on Pearl Harbor. Isoroku Yamamoto graduated from the Japanese naval academy in 1904 and started his climb to the top. In 1925, he was assigned to the Japanese embassy in Washington. While in Washington he met and started to associate with a number of Christians. He was able to talk his Christian friends into lifting the ban on the construction of battleships that was preventing the Japanese navy from growing. By 1941, the Japanese navy was ready for their attack on Pearl Harbor. Yamamoto was the one that planned the attack on Pearl Harbor, and with its success he was considered invincible. The fabricated story again held that the Christians were the ones responsible for the attack on Pearl Harbor. If they had not allowed Yamamoto to build battleships, the Japanese Navy would never have attacked.

"The Vietnam War and the Gulf Wars were also claimed to be the work of Christians. John Kennedy claimed to be a Christian, and he was the President who sent our troops into Vietnam.

"Iraq would not have invaded Kuwait if the Christians had not talked the Kuwaits into not listening to what Iraq had to say. It was just one war after another that the Christians were responsible for, and now they were gone. It was really funny how people back in those days thought whatever they read in the newspapers or on their computers was the truth.

"As I stated before, heads of governments also disappeared. The President and Vice President of the United States disappeared that morning also. John Alexander Steele was elected President in 2008. He was one of the most conservative Presidents ever, and his Vice President, Benjamin Moses Brown, was more conservative than the President.

"John Steele was black, but the 73 percent of the people who voted for him were mostly white. A large number of the blacks did not like the programs he wanted to put in. They called him an Uncle Tom. He had received his degree from Princeton and received his Masters and Doctorate from Princeton also. As I stated before, he was a very conservative Christian Republican.

"Benjamin Moses Brown, as you might assume by his name, was a Christian. He was raised in a Christian family and went to a Christian University.

"Their relationship started back in 2000. Both were

elected to the Senate the same year and became very good friends. The two did everything together, as did their wives and children. Their popularity grew and in 2006, they decided to run for the highest office in the land. Ben knew he could pull a very large number of white votes and John could pull some of the black votes, along with white and Hispanic votes.

"Everything was going along just fine until July of 2008. Ben had a massive heart attack. For three days they did not know if he would live or die. He did recover, but he knew if the Republicans were to win the election, he could not run as President. A news conference was called, and Ben said John decided the best thing for the country and the party was for John to run as President, and he would run as Vice President.

"Nothing like that had ever happened before. If they won the election, John would be the first black President in the history of the United States.

"During the debates, John, who had a photographic memory, gave facts and figures that totally left his opponent speechless. The two areas they thought would cause problems were prayer in school and the abortion issue. His opponent was pro-abortion, and John had made it known, if he was elected, he would outlaw all abortions. Secondly, he had stated he would do everything in his power to restore optional prayer in school. Anyone would have a right to pray wherever and whenever they wanted.

"A third point in the debates he included would be letting the public know of his attempt to develop some plan that would keep the fathers in the home or bring them back.

"Along with those three items, the fourth was also very important. Crime was so rampant in the country, they wanted to put more than 200,000 new officers on the streets. Also, he wanted to replace all the judges who gave light sentences to criminals. He wanted to make it clear, 'If you do the crime, you will do the time.' He stated that these four issues were the things that were destroying our country. We had to have a change.

"After all the debates, John and Ben were so far ahead in the polls, they would be a shoe-in. The public agreed with what John had said. They wanted a change and with John and Ben, they knew they were going to get that change.

"Immediately after being sworn in, they started to make the changes that would turn the United States around. Not knowing if he had the votes in the Senate or in the House of Representatives, he put together four bills.

"The first outlawed all abortion. The second would allow prayer back in schools. The third was a mandatory bill that would make everyone serve at least five years in prison if convicted of a felony. The fourth and most controversial was a plan that would keep fathers in their homes.

"This fourth bill would require all couples to have 24 hours of counseling before they could obtain a divorce. If a divorce was granted, and there were children involved, the father had to pay for child support or he would be sent to prison. One bill after another passed, and within six months, things had turned around in the United States.

"The United States had been on the road to social disaster, until the four bills passed. After two years of changes, there was a complete reverse. The crime rate was the lowest it had been in 20 years. Murders, armed robberies, petty theft and all other areas of crime were down.

"The only crime that continued to rise was road rage. Once a person got behind the wheel of a car, they thought they owned the road. The new highway system that had been planned to start in 2012 should put a halt to the road rage. The new highway system would have electric metal plates in the middle of each lane of traffic. Every new car made in 2012 and beyond would be equipped with a sensor device that would direct the car to its destination. In other words, the driver did not drive the car any more. Road rage should come to a stop once everyone had the new cars. It may take three or four years, but they knew the system would work.

"Even though the bills which John and Ben worked on to change things in the U.S. worked, they did not change the world. The problems in the world remained. The biggest problem the world was facing was terrorism. John and Ben both were threatened, and one plot to shoot John in England was discovered just in time. There were talks held at the United Nations on how to stop the terrorists' attacks world-wide. Well, that is about all they did, talk. Everyone knew the United Nations was just a joke. John put forth one bill after another to the Senate to have the U.N. removed from the U.S., but all attempts failed.

"Something had to be done about terrorism, but what? Different ideas were proposed but nothing, it seemed, would work. Nothing was going to work, that is, until Michael made the announcement three days after the rapture, that he had a plan and it would work. He said he would reveal the plan to the world within weeks. 'A plan that would work to stop terrorist acts in the world must be a dream,' people thought. What could possibly keep someone from committing that type of crime?

"The Russians had one plan that probably would

have worked, but all the delegates in the United Nations voted it down. The plan was simple. If the person who performs the act of terrorism is discovered, their entire family would be put to death. Everyone from the oldest to the youngest.

"A plan similar to that worked when three Russian diplomats were kidnapped in Spain. They would be released if 50 prisoners that were being held by the U.S. were released. If they were not released, the three diplomats from Russia would die and their blood would be on the hands of the Americans. The four terrorists that were holding the Russians were all from Libya.

"The Russians sent their secret police into Libya and kidnapped the entire family of one of the terrorist. At an isolated location everyone in that family was murdered, and the video was sent to the terrorist. While the video was en route, the Russians kidnapped everyone in the other three families. The ultimatum was to release the diplomats or the same thing would happen to the other three families. As soon as the terrorists viewed the video, they released the diplomats. The United Nations said the Russian idea was too barbaric.

"With the disappearance of hundreds of millions throughout the world, maybe terrorist acts would stop. After all, it was the undesirables who were the terrorists. Well, that was a good thought, but the day after the rapture, Tom and Debbie were almost killed by an attack on Michael's mansion in Rome. Tom and Debbie were lucky Michael had decided to triple the security around all the homes he owned and around all his places of business. In the last three years, there had been a number of threats against his life, but he never took them seriously. He now considered any threat very serious. He was going to stop terrorism in the world, and he knew exactly how to do it.

"The newspapers continued to have stories on the front page about those who had disappeared, but the headlines were starting to tell more of the peace talks in the Middle East. If peace is worked out, it could bring peace to the entire world. Everyone had their fingers crossed and hoped that the Prince of Peace could work another miracle. Reporters were asking the same questions, 'Why have a peace treaty if it means nothing? If Israel and the Arab nations sign a peace treaty today, what would prevent the Arabs from hitting Israel with a surprise attack one week from now or one year from now?' This peace treaty had to be a long-term agreement. Israel also wanted a long-term agreement. She wanted some type of guarantee that would protect her from the Arab nations. For the first time since Israel became a nation, peace, real peace, was at hand.

"Ten days after the rapture, most people said nothing about the missing people. It was taken for granted the missing would never return. Things had settled down and people were doing their everyday jobs again. The only thing that was void were churches. Almost all the people who went to Bible-believing churches on Sundays were gone. The ones who were left had no reason to go back to church. The few people that did go back were frightened. They knew what had been taught in the sermons and now believed the true believers were gone. In some churches the pastor was still there, along with some of the deacons. Other churches that did not believe in the fundamentals of the faith lost almost no members at all. The theory of a rapture was soon dispelled. The only thing that was known for sure was the people who were called Christians were gone."

CHAPTER 15

"THE RAPTURE occurred on Thursday, February 17, 2011. On the next Monday, Michael met with Israel and the delegates from the Arab confederacy to discuss peace. Before the talks started, the speaker for the Arab confederacy said they would like to have someone else be the negotiator of the peace talks. They said they checked on Michael's background and found that his grandmother was an orthodox Jew. Also, he had gone to Jewish schools all his life. They knew he was pro-Israeli, and if the talks were to be a success, Michael would have to leave. Michael said he was offended by the statements his Arab brother had just made.

"One delegate stood up and said, 'You are not our brother!'

"Michael said, 'That has been the story of my life. My grandmother was an orthodox Jew. She married my grandfather, Omar Hassan. My grandfather was killed in a car accident before I was born. My father, mother, brother and sister died in a fire when I was a small boy. I went to live with my grandmother and my step-grandfather. When I was old enough to start to school, my grandmother put me in a Jewish school. The kids did not accept me because they said I was not Jewish. When they found out my grandfather was an Arab from Jordan, I was an outcast in the Jewish community. Yes, all through my life I went to Jewish schools and I received my degree from Hebrew University, but that does not change my blood. I am one-fourth Jewish and one-fourth Arab. You say I am not your brother? What kind of blood must I have in order to be an Arab. My great-grandfather was the most decorated soldier in the Jordanian army, Kamiel Hassan. He became a General and was the person responsible for Jordan joining the Arab war against Israel in 1967. I now ask if there is anyone here who says I am not an Arab or a Jew?'

"There was total silence, no one said a word, and there were never any remarks about Michael not being an Arab or Jewish again.

"The talk in the newspapers and on TV was the fact that there had to be some long-term peace agreement, or the peace would be a paper peace only. Michael gave both sides a chance to write down all the points of their terms and then they could focus on each point.

"The Arabs wrote down their points and then began to talk about the first point with Israel. The first point the Arabs insisted on concerned the Golan Heights. They wanted to have full control of the Golan Heights. The Israelis said no immediately. The Arabs said there was no reason to talk peace if Israel was going to say no on every point.

"Michael said to read all the points, then they would talk. The Arabs restated they wanted the Golan Heights. The second point stated the building of new settlements would have to stop. Each side would have their delegates meet and talk about the building of new settlements first. If Israel built a settlement for their people, they would have to build a settlement for the Arabs also. The third point would be fair employment in Israel for Arabs. There could be no discrimination by Jewish business owners. The fourth point was to make Jerusalem an international city. The fifth point would be the destruction of all nuclear bombs Israel had hidden. Michael asked if there were any other points, and the Arab delegate said those were the points that would bring peace from their viewpoint.

"The delegate for Israel then stated their points. The first point was to have a wall built that would separate the Dome of The Rock from the place the Jews wanted to build a temple. The second point was for a public statement from every Arab country that signed the peace treaty, that they would recognize Israel as a country. The third point would be for all calendars to go back to the Old Testament days when there were 30 days in a month. The fourth point was that Israel could begin animal sacrifices as soon as the temple was built, and there would be no retribution for the killing of animals. The fifth point was that Israel wanted some kind of long-term agreement that would guarantee the peace. The sixth point was to put the Ark in the new temple.

"Michael said, 'We have the points of discussion on the table. We can now talk. I will meet tomorrow with Israel and discuss the Arab points, and the following day I will meet with the Arabs and discuss the Israeli points.'

"When Michael was on his way home, he received a telephone call from Dr. Messenger. He told Michael the screening committee from the ECU called and wanted him to call them immediately, if possible. He said he would be home in five minutes and would call at that time. With Dr. Messenger seated nearby, Michael called the chairman of the screening committee. They talked about the peace treaty and if there was truly going to be peace. Michael said, 'There will be peace, we just have to work out the problem areas.'

" 'The real reason I called was to ask if you would be interested in becoming the new president of the ECU?'

"Michael paused for a moment and said, 'I would be

interested in that position, but the ECU has an agenda of war. I am a man of peace. If the ECU made a public statement denouncing war and if they were going to undertake an agenda of peace, I would accept the position of president.'

"The chairman said, 'I will have to talk to all the delegates and see what their thoughts are about that type of statement.'

"Michael reminded him, 'I am known as the Prince of Peace, and if it was public knowledge that the ECU has asked me to become president and yet was not willing to take a stand for peace, it could have worldwide repercussions.' With that statement the chairman knew he was in a position that would be very hard to get out of.

"The chairman spoke with the 11 delegates from the nations that formed the European Common Market to see if they had changed their minds about asking Michael to be president. He told them, 'Michael wants a public statement that would put the ECU on an agenda of peace. These are his terms of acceptance.' The result was the same as it was when they first talked. Eight delegates were still voting to have Michael sworn in as president and three delegates were totally opposed. The ECU always went with the majority, and it would be no different at this time. Michael would be asked to take over as president of the European Common Market.

"The next day the chairman called and told Michael the delegates had agreed to make a statement that would usher in a time of peace. He said he wanted Michael to come to Brussels so he could be sworn in on Thursday. Michael said he would ask for a pause in the peace talks, and hopefully everyone would understand.

"The following day Michael called for both parties to

return to the peace table. He said, 'Something has come up that will ensure peace, but I must be gone for a couple of days, and when I get back on Friday the talks will resume."

"On the plane to Brussels, Dr. Messenger told Michael, 'The things we had planned are all starting to work out. The world is at our feet. When you meet with the delegates, make sure you remind them of the peace talks and that the ECU must guarantee the peace of Israel or there will be war. Also, let them know you want the ECU to be the strongest union of countries in the world, economically. All the countries of the world must trade with either gold or the ECU dollar.'

"When Michael met with the delegates at the headquarters in Brussels, he explained to them what was going on at the peace talks. He said, 'Israel is demanding that the ECU guarantee her safety.'

"One delegate asked, 'How can the ECU guarantee the safety of Israel?'

"Michael explained, 'It is very easy, if any country attacks Israel, it is the same as an attack on the ECU.' The three delegates who were opposed to Michael becoming president were also against the ECU protecting Israel. Michael did not let those three delegates know how mad he was, but he determined he was going to get rid of them as soon as he could come up with a good plan. The other eight delegates agreed the best way to avoid war would be to guarantee the peace of Israel. Michael also gave them his idea how the ECU could become stronger than any group of nations in the world, economically. He said, 'If they want to do business with us, they must use gold or our dollar.'

The three delegates said, 'That would mean the only currency in the world is our dollar.'

"Michael said, 'That's exactly right.'

"They said, 'The other countries will not stand for it.'

"At that time, Michael informed them he was the inventor and the owner of the only computer system in the world. 'If the other countries want to do business with us, they will have to do what we say. I will pull the plug on any country that resists, and without the use of computers I will bring them to their knees.'

"The three delegates who were against him thought to themselves, 'This does not sound like the Prince of Peace talking, it sounds more like a person who is wanting to take over the world.' The vote was taken, and it was eight to three. What Michael wanted, he got. At five in the afternoon, Michael was sworn into office as the president of the Common Market.

"Michael and Dr. Messenger flew back to Jerusalem that night and were ready for the peace talks the next morning. Upon arriving at the peace conference, all the delegates stood and congratulated Michael. He informed them they had to have a firm agreement for peace before April. 'If we have to take 10 or 12 hours a day until peace is worked out, we will do it. I want to have the peace treaty signed on April 3.' The delegates wondered why he wanted everything finalized and the treaty signed on April 3.

"If you remember, I told you that I had told Michael many things about the rapture and that there would be a 45-day lull period before the tribulation. When the rapture occurred on February 17, he knew the tribulation had to begin on April 3. It could not be a day earlier or a day later; it had to be on the 3rd. Michael did not fully understand why the signing had to be on that date; if he had, he would not have signed on April 3.

"Twelve-hundred and sixty days after Michael signed

the treaty, he would go into the temple and proclaim himself to be God. I had told you before that date would be October 3, 2014. That date was Yom Kippur. Michael was going to do everything in his power to hasten the peace talks. Day after day the peace talks continued. Michael thought it might be best if they took a couple of days off and rest.

"The ECU officials were getting a little agitated that their president was in Jerusalem instead of in Brussels. When called, Michael made it perfectly clear that this peace treaty would bring peace to the world. If it meant he would have to stay away for 30 days or more, it would be worth it. Michael knew the three delegates who had opposed him were the ones complaining. He thought to himself, 'As soon as we sign the peace treaty, you three are going to get the surprise of your lives.'

"The night before the peace talks resumed, Dr. Messenger and Michael talked for two hours about the different points Michael would make the next day. Dr. Messenger said it would be better to announce the guarantee as the first point. Since Egypt and the other Arab countries signed their mutual protection accord, which they call the Southern Confederacy, to guarantee the protection of Israel may be an insult to them. 'If you get by the first point without anyone saying anything about it, the other points will pass. But the way the point is worded, they will think it is leaning towards them.'

"At the peace table, each side discussed the different points which they wanted. Israel would not give up the Golan Heights even for peace. The Arabs would not change their mind; they wanted the Golan Heights. Michael said he had come up with a 10-point peace plan that both parties could live with. He then started to give each point.

" 'Point one, the ECU will guarantee the peace of Israel for seven years. If there is an attack on Israel, it will be the same as an attack on the European Common Market, and everyone remembers what happened to Iran in 2008. We will place 300,000 troops in Israel to guarantee her peace. The troops will be placed in every city and in every town. If there is an attack, the attackers will have to kill ECU troops first, and that will bring an immediate response from the ECU.

" 'The second point is, since we are going to defend Israel, Israel will have to give up all her weapons of war. This includes all her nuclear bombs. This plan will help Israel economically. She will not have to spend any money on war machines or on war material. All of those billions of dollars can be used to set up social programs for the Jews and the Arabs.

" 'The third point is to set up the guillotine as the only method of capital punishment. The threat of terrorism will not be halted unless we eliminate the terrorists. If we are going to use the guillotine for terrorism, we should also use it for all types of capital crime. When a person is caught in the act of a crime, they will appear in front of a special judge. That judge will be appointed, and his identity will not be revealed. If we reveal who he is, he could be assassinated. The person caught in the act will be tried within 24 hours, and if found guilty by the judge, that person will have his head cut off in a public execution. The guillotine will be set up in every city and town in Israel.

" 'The fourth point relates to the Golan Heights. Israel will give up the control of the Golan Heights to the Arabs. Since Israel is giving up all her weapons of war, the Arabs who live in Israel will have to do the same. The only troops that will have any weapons will be ECU troops. The Golan Heights will continue to be part of Israel, and since it will be part of Israel, there will be no weapons allowed in that area either. If any country attempts or does bring weapons into the Golan Heights, it will be the same as an attack on the ECU. The Golan Heights will be open territory to both Arabs and Jews. If there are any disputes in the Golan Heights, the special judge who is appointed for that area will determine which side is correct, and his judgment will be final.

" 'The fifth point deals with the temple mount. The Dome of The Rock will remain where it is, and there will be no changes in the control of that area. There will be a wall built next to the Dome which will be five feet taller than the highest point on the Dome. The wall will extent the full length of the area next to the Dome. The Jews will be able to build their temple where they consider to be the Holy Place. Their temple cannot be higher than the highest point on the Dome. The Ark will be placed inside the temple, and it cannot be removed for any reason. The animal sacrifices will begin when the temple is finished. If Israel agrees to do away with her weapons of war, I will match whatever money she uses on the temple. If she were to put $500 million into the building of the temple, I will also put $500 million in for the building of the temple. All calendars will be changed to the Old Testament days of Israel. There will be 30 days per month starting in April.

" 'The sixth point is to recognize Jerusalem as an International City. Since Jerusalem will be an International City, it will be governed by International Rules. What this means is that every country in the world will have to have an ambassador in Jerusalem, under the agreement signed by all countries of the world in 2007. Each country will have to give the government of Jerusalem $1 million a year. Also, every foreigner who comes to Jerusalem after the signing will have to pay a 10 percent tax on everything they buy. Also, if any item is brought into Jerusalem, it will be assessed the ten percent tax.

" 'The seventh point will be that the Arabs have the right to work in Israel without being discriminated against by Jewish business owners. If anyone is discriminated against, that place of business will be shut down by the agreement signed in 2007.

" 'The eighth point concerns the building of settlements. Israel can continue to build settlements only if they build equal settlements for the Arabs. One-fifth of the money Israel would have used on war materials will be used to build settlements. Dr. Messenger said he would match whatever money is used to build new settlements for both the Arabs and the Jews.

" 'The ninth point would be a $50 tariff for every person entering Israel. The tax would be paid only once a year. That money will be used to build a rail system throughout Israel. If the surrounding countries want to connect to Israel's rail system, they will have to pay a tax.

" 'The tenth point, the Arab countries that sign the peace treaty will have to acknowledge, in public, that the nation of Israel has the right to exist.'

"After giving his 10-point peace treaty to both sides, he stated he had been as fair as he could be to both sides. He asked for a two-day rest so both sides could talk with each country's officials. He informed both sides that the news media was wanting to know what the points of peace were. 'There will be a news conference called in one hour, and at that time I will give the 10-point peace plan to the world.'

"Michael gave the media exactly what it wanted, the

10-point peace plan. The questions came fast and furious. Question after question was asked, until Michael put a halt to the mad rush. He said, 'One question at a time, please.'

"The first question asked was about peace. 'Will this peace treaty really stop the war between the Jews and the Arabs?'

"Michael smiled and said, 'Yes, it will. But it goes a step further. The world will see how peace is supposed to be, and this agreement will bring in world-wide peace within 3-1/2 years.'

"The next question focused on who was to gain, the Arabs or the Jews? Michael answered that question very easily. 'Both sides gain. I don't see how either side can say they lost face or territory. Both sides will gain a lot, and neither side will be a loser.'

"One reporter was stumped, so he asked Michael a question. The reporter wanted to know, 'Whose idea is it to have one of the points to be the rail system? That does not seem to have much to do with peace.'

"Michael said, 'That is my idea. If Israel and the Arabs build new settlements, that will mean more people, and with more people there will be more jobs. With a rail system people can go from small towns to larger towns or cities to find work. Also, with Jerusalem becoming an International City, it will bring a lot of tourists into the country. The tourists can go anywhere in Israel very quickly. Just think, if the surrounding countries were to tie into the rail system, the tourist who comes to Jerusalem can take a train to Cairo or some other large city, and that would help the surrounding Arab countries economically. If tourists wanted to see the countryside, they would be able to take a train and visit Petra, if Jordan were connected to the system. Not only could Israel make a lot of money out of the tourist trade, but so could the surrounding countries. And as we all know, money is often the cause of conflicts.'

"Another reporter asked about the guarantee. Michael made it perfectly clear that Israel would become totally defenseless. 'She has to be protected even if it means a world war. If she signs the agreement, she promises to do away with all weapons of war. Using a term from the Old Testament, Israel will be living in unwalled cities.'

"The next question was about the guillotine. 'Do you really think that the guillotine will stop crime?'

"Michael said, 'I don't know if it will stop crime or terrorist or anything. But I know this, that if a person is a terrorist or a criminal and is caught, he will be holding his head in his hands within 24 hours. I believe it will stop all types of crimes immediately. The humiliation a person and the family would experience by a public execution would be unthinkable. Yes, the guillotine will stop crime. Just think, if the crime rate goes down to nothing in Israel, the other countries throughout the world will probably put in the guillotine as their method of capital punishment, also.'

"One reporter asked a question about money. 'Michael, you and Dr. Messenger have promised to match whatever money is used on the temple and on the building of settlements. That is a lot of money out of your own pockets to spend just for peace.'

" 'That is correct, but sometimes you have to spend a lot to get a lot. The price of peace cannot be measured by money, but peace can be measured by the number of lives it saves. If I had to spend all I had for peace in the Middle East, I would spend it. That is the last question I will entertain. I need to get some rest.' He was dead tired.

"The next morning the headlines read, 'PEACE IN THE MIDDLE EAST?' The talk everywhere was peace. People were talking about the 10-point plan. The radio talk shows were talking about peace. On TV, all programs were put on hold while different reporters had experts giving their ideas about the 10-point plan. All over the world the talk was positive about the talks.

"The Russian news media stopped all programming to tell the country about the Middle East situation. They seemed delighted that Israel would be giving up all her nuclear bombs and other weapons of war. One General was interviewed and asked what he thought about Israel giving up all her weapons. He said sarcastically, 'It is really a shame that Israel is going to be defenseless. Any country could invade her.' The more the Russians talked, the more it seemed as if the Russians were acting like a wolf about to devour a lamb. Russia was as strong now as she was before the end of the Cold War.

"The treaty she signed with Iran right after the ECU's surprise attack in 2008 was the start of the rebuilding of the Russian war machine. The treaty stated that an attack on Iran would be the same as an attack on Russia. Iran had to give the Russians $5 billion for that agreement. The money was needed so badly that Russia started making the same agreement with other nations. Iraq decided it was in her best interest to join Russia and Iran. But the Russians saw what was going to happen and the price for Iraq would be $6 billion. The third country that wanted Russian backing was Libya. Libya and the other countries that paid Russia were already allies of Russia, except for Germany. The other countries never had a firm treaty signed, but money can do wonders. Ethiopia was the next country to sign, then came Turkey and Germany.

"The Germans were part of the European Common Market but were kicked out because of her neo-Nazi backing. The German government had high-ranking officials that were outspoken backers of the neo-Nazi party. The scandal was growing larger and larger, and finally the ECU said that was enough. By a majority vote, Germany was expelled. The German government decided the Northern Confederacy was going to be a major power in the world, and it would be best to be with the Russians rather than against them. The Russians made over $40 billion from all the countries that wanted Russian protection.

"It was obvious, the Northern Confederacy was preparing for war, but where would war break out? The Russians were looking at Israel, but as long as Israel had nuclear bombs, Russia would not invade. If the Russians did invade Israel, it would have to face the ECU army, which was also backed by the United States. With the United States and the ECU armies together, it would be almost impossible for any country or group of countries to win against those odds. The Russians would just sit and wait for the right moment.

"The delegate to the peace talks for Israel convened with his officials, and they discussed the 10-point plan. All the officials stated they did not see any problems with any of the points. The Golan Heights was a major sticking point, but the way the treaty read, if any country put weapons in that area, it would be an attack on the ECU. The way Michael had put it together, the other points looked as if he was pro-Israeli. Making Jerusalem an International City was not what the people wanted, but the way the point read it was the best thing for Jerusalem and Israel. 'The money Dr. Messenger is going to give to help build settlements for both the Arabs and us is an answer to prayer. Plus the money to help build the temple that Michael is going to give will ensure the most magnificent temple since Solomon's. Every point leans toward the Israeli point of view.'

"The Arab delegates met with their officials also. They went over every point with a fine-tooth comb. They all agreed the points leaned toward the Arabs' point of view. The one delegate who said Michael was not an Arab confessed he was totally wrong. 'Michael is an Arab, and the 10-point peace treaty shows that he is a true brother."

"After a two-day rest, the peace conference reconvened. Michael asked if everyone was able to go over each point with their officials. They all agreed they had talked everything over. Michael wanted to know what the Israeli government believed about the peace plans. The delegate said his government thought the points were as good as could be expected and they would sign. He asked the Arab delegates, and their response was the same as the Israeli delegates. The Arabs would sign the peace treaty also.

"Michael said he would draw up the official papers and have them ready for each party to sign on April 3, 2011, at 10 in the morning. He said he was going to contact a friend at one of the largest TV networks and make sure the signing was covered world-wide. He said he also wanted the signing to be heard on all the radio stations. 'Since Dr. Messenger is going to put up a large amount of money, I would like to have him there at the signing. At the signing, each country's delegate will sign the peace treaty and acknowledge that Israel has a right to exist. After each country has signed the treaty, the 10-point plan will be read over the air, so the people of the world will know there is peace in the Middle East.'

"At the end of the day, Michael and Dr. Messenger

went back to Michael's home. At the house they started to discuss how they could get rid of three officials of the ECU. 'We know we can't blow up a plane they are on; that would look too suspicious since the other plane accident took high officials. We know we can't use a scandal against them; we used that before. Instead of killing all three at one time, it may be best to eliminate them one at a time.' Michael said it might be best to wait until after the peace treaty was signed. Dr. Messenger agreed it would be better to take care of business first, and then take care of personal business or fun next.

"The day the whole world had been waiting for was at hand. Heads of State from every country in the world were there to watch the historic signing.

"The one block of countries that Michael thought he would have a lot of problems with sometime in the future was the Eastern Confederacy. During the last two or three years, all the countries of the world had been lining up behind one major power or another for protection. When the United States pulled out of the Far East, it left one major power, China. The other countries around her decided it was in their best interest to have China as an ally rather than an enemy. Japan was the first to sign an agreement with China and after that, it was one country after another. Within one year, almost all of the Far East countries had signed with China. The Chinese army alone could field an army of over 200 million soldiers. However, with the other countries' combined armies, they were well over 200 million soldiers strong. Michael knew one of these days he might have to fight the Eastern Confederacy.

"As he looked at the different officials who came into the large meeting room, he knew all the eyes of the world were focused on him. This day was his day. He was the one everyone was watching. He was the 'Prince of Peace.' Peace for the whole world was at hand. One official after another came into the room and had a seat.

"Once everyone was seated, Dr. Messenger rose and walked to the microphone. He spoke very eloquently and told how much time Michael had spent putting this peace treaty together. 'Sleepless nights, the telephone calls to work out this point or that point, the long days of talks, and going back and forth from one location to another were tiring. Because of all the hard work that Michael has put forth, we have a peace treaty that will usher in peace around the world. At this time, I want to introduce the world to Michael D. Glispbe, The Prince of Peace.'

"Michael arose and walked to the podium. Dr. Messenger did something that had been done only once to Michael before. Dr. Messenger kneeled down and kissed his right hand. Michael was caught off guard by Dr. Messenger. He did not know what to say or to do. He stood at the microphone, waiting for the cheering and the applause to stop. But they did not stop. They continued for one minute, then two minutes, and five minutes later it was still going on. Finally, Michael spoke into the microphone. Everyone stopped cheering and applauding and took their seats.

"Michael said, 'This is the most important day in the history of the world. This day will be spoken of for years to come. This day we have peace in the Middle East. Tomorrow we will have peace in the world!' With that statement, everyone stood and cheered. After two minutes of cheers, Michael spoke again and said, 'The start of peace in the world started when Dr. Messenger set up the Brotherhood of Common Beliefs. The Brotherhood was set up to stop wars before they begin.

" 'At this time, I would like to have all the countries

involved in the peace signing to come forward. Israel will sign the treaty first and then the other countries will sign, and after each of those countries sign they will make a short comment.'

"After Israel signed the treaty, then came Egypt, the leader of the Southern Confederacy. When the Egyptian official signed the treaty, he walked to the microphone and stated to the whole world, 'Israel has the right to exist as a nation.' Country after country signed the treaty and made the same statement.

"When everyone was finished signing, Michael signed his name to the peace treaty and walked to the microphone and said, **'These proceedings are closed.'** With his signature, the dreaded Day of the Lord began. No one had any idea what was in store for the world for the next seven years. The time known as the Tribulation would change everything, and the world would not be the same again."

CHAPTER 16

"**I KNOW THERE** must be a lot of questions at this time, so I will try and answer all your questions. Alan, what is your question?"

"You said the Russians were waiting for the right time to attack Israel. Did they attack Israel?"

"Yes. When they attacked Israel, World War Three began. I will tell you more about World War Three in the months to come. Randy, what is your question?"

"Did Dr. Messenger like Dr. Mohammed?"

"The answer to that question is NO! Dr. Messenger despised Dr. Mohammed. Let me talk about these two right now.

"Dr. Mohammed was intent on having his religion 'the religion' of the world. He did not care what anyone thought or what anyone said, he wanted the world to have that which was perfect. His religion was the most perfect religion the world had ever seen. Well, in his eyes he could say that. The real truth was his religion fell short of what a perfect religion should be. However, he wanted his religion to be the most important in the world. He did not care if he had to compromise a little in order to gain a lot. When Dr. Messenger said he was moving his headquarters to Babylon, Dr. Mohammed was thinking of ways he could influence or sway Dr. Messenger into the way he was thinking.

"Dr. Messenger was thinking the same thing. 'If I move my headquarters to Babylon, I could be closer to

Dr. Mohammed and I would have a chance to influence him.' The more influence he had with Dr. Mohammed, the more he thought he could change the thinking of Dr. Mohammed. Sooner or later, Dr. Mohammed and the new religion would conform to Dr. Messenger's ideas. Well, it never happened. The more influence Dr. Messenger exerted on Dr. Mohammed, the more Dr. Mohammed resisted.

"That is when Michael and Dr. Messenger knew they had to remove the obstacle. On that day in February, the obstacle was removed. If you remember, I told you of the bomb that was placed on the ECU jet that killed Dr. Mohammed and the top officials of the ECU.

"The Board of Directors of the Fellowship of Believers met with the intent of asking Dr. Messenger to be their new spiritual leader. He said it would be an honor to be the spiritual leader of the only true church in the world. In his inner thoughts, Dr. Messenger knew there was no one else as qualified as he was. And if they did not select him, he would start to eliminate those who were opposed to him. One thing about Michael and Dr. Messenger, if anyone opposed them, they would just have them removed, permanently. The Board asked him when he would like to take over as the new head of the religion. He said he thought it would be best for him to be installed immediately, but on April 4 he wanted to have a public commission in front of the whole world. 'On April 3, Michael is going to be signing the peace treaty, and I am supposed to be with him at that time. In order for the church to receive as much publicity as possible, I will have Michael with me at the commissioning services, also. By having the president of the World — oh, I mean, the president of the European Common Market present, the news media from all over the world will be at the commissioning services.' The Board members thought it was a good idea and decided to install Dr. Messenger before the day was out. They had not caught his slip of the tongue.

"Dr. Messenger was now the head of the church that the Bible said would be the counterfeit church in the tribulation. He immediately started to change things so the church could take in the other churches of the world. He first put forth certain statements that would be announced on April 5.

"The first statement was, 'There is only one god, and every religion has the same god. In each religion we call him by a different name, but he is still the same god. If every religion has the same god, then why have all these different religions? The Bible says, *And the Word was made flesh, and dwelt among us and we beheld his glory, the glory as of the only begotten, full of grace and truth.* This prophecy has never been fulfilled, but I am going to predict within 3-1/2 years God will reveal himself to us in a man. That man is god. As I said, every religion has used a different name for god, but his real name is Neanias. I want every religion in the world to start using his real name. If you do not use his real name now, when he comes, he will reject that religion and everyone in that religion, for not calling him by his real name.' The religions of the world believed what Dr. Messenger said and every person was calling god 'Neanias.' They also believed the prediction of Dr. Messenger.

"The news medias and people all over the world were talking about the soon coming of god. If the people knew what the Greek word Neanias meant, they would have known the word does not mean god. In the Greek, Neanias means a youth not yet 40 years of age. Michael was going to fulfill Dr. Messenger's prophecy. When Michael did fulfill Dr. Messenger's prophecy, the world was turned upside down. Mankind would be facing extinction on planet earth in the coming years. The plans Michael and Dr. Messenger prepared worked, and they would continue to work until the end of the tribulation.

"The second statement Dr. Messenger made was about the headquarters of all the religions of the world. 'Since every religion has the same god, then every religion should have one central location. I had our giant computer search the world over for the center of the world. The computer said the center of the world is located in Iraq. And to be more specific, the center of the world is at the very site of the headquarters known as the Fellowship of Believers. I believe a central location for all the world religions should be located at the center of the world. We did not have to have the computer to tell us the center of the world is in Babylon. We should have known the center was located here because of the true story of the Tower of Babel.

" 'The Tower of Babel was built on the location that was the center of the world. Nimrod was building a tower or a monument to Neanias. The people became embittered by their hard work and started to rebel. Nimrod explained to the people the tower was going to be a place where they could worship god. But the people did not want any part of a god that made them work so hard. The rebellion made Neanias mad, and he said if they will not worship me I will confuse their language. The building of the tower had to stop and a place to worship god was never built.

" 'I want to make the headquarters of The Fellowship of Believers building the new headquarters for all the religions of the world. I also want to change the name to the Fellowship of World Believers. I know all the religions of the world will want to be a part of this new movement. I want every religion to have their top two religious leaders here for an introduction to the world. Over world TV, I will introduced each representative of that religion and where the religion is located. Everyone in the world will be watching this very important broadcast.'

"Every religion sent their representatives to Babylon. The announcement would be seen and heard all over the world, and it would put all the representatives in the limelight; that was something that had never happened to any of them before.

"The third statement from Dr. Messenger was, 'Everyone should be proud of their new religion. The only way for you to be proud of the new religion is to have a mark showing you believe in the new religion and you believe Neanias is god. The mark will be a lapel pen that should be worn on the collar of your shirt or blouse. When anyone sees the lapel pen, they will know that you are a fellow believer. If you do not wear your pen, you will be considered as an outcast. The emblem on the pen will be a woman riding upon a dragon. The woman represents our world church, and the dragon represents our strength. The strength of the dragon is known world-wide. Our church will be like the dragon; we will be strong. I want all businesses to look to see if the person being interviewed for that new job is a believer. If he has his pen on, then you know he is a believer. If he does not have his pen on, you may ask if he has a pen or if he is not a believer. I cannot say you should not hire that person if they are not a believer, but having people who believe the same thing could cut down on friction within the work area. It is possible that one of these days it will be the law that you must have a mark in order to buy, sell or to have a job. I am sure that time is well into the future. Just think, if you get used to wearing your pen as a sign of your belief, perhaps someday if you are asked to take a mark to prove your belief, it won't be a big deal.'

"Dr. Messenger had the approval of the Board of Directors for all the changes and for the lapel pen. They thought the pen idea was something they should have thought of years before. One of the Board members said, 'If Dr. Mohammed could see what is happening, he would not believe it.' That statement was true; if Dr. Mohammed could see all the changes, he would roll over in his grave.

"The way Dr. Messenger was setting everything up, it would be easy for Michael to proclaim himself to be god. But in order for the world to accept Michael, there would have to be some kind of fake miracle to make the world believe he was god. Plus, there would have to be scripture to prove Michael was God. Dr. Messenger was a genius when it came to taking a verse out of context. He could twist the scriptures to make it say anything he wanted it to say. His story about the Tower of Babel was one good example. Also, there was no one checking to see what the scriptures really said anyway. So Dr. Messenger could say anything without fear of being caught. Also, if he was caught, he could always say he was the expert. Who would they believe, someone trying to cause trouble or Dr. Messenger?

"Dr. Messenger met with Michael and said everything was set up just the way we had planned. The changes would take place right after the peace signing on April 3. 'The world will be ours without anyone knowing what happened.'

"Michael said the date for the launch of the new satellite would be April 2, and it should go into orbit on the third. 'By the time we sign the peace treaty, all the satellites should be functional.'

"Dr. Messenger asked, 'Michael, are you sure the

secret covering over the satellites made them invisible to scanners and/or radar?'

"Michael said, 'I checked the solution, time and time again, to make sure it worked, and each time I used a scanner the scanner could not detect the metal. I also checked it with radar, and the radar could not detect any metal either. With our other satellites in orbit, no one will know where the fire balls are coming from. If we need to use the secret weapon after the third, it will be available.'

"Dr. Messenger responded, 'If you have to use the weapon, make sure there are a number of people watching. Also make the statement, 'I am going to call fire down from heaven and consume my enemies.'

"Michael agreed to everything Dr. Messenger said; then he started to laugh and laugh and laugh. Dr. Messenger asked what he was laughing about, and Michael said, 'Can you image my enemies trying to harm me or kill me and in a loud voice I call down fire from heaven? As they stand there, they don't believe I can call fire down from heaven, but then comes this loud sound of the fire, and all of a sudden my enemies are consumed. I think that is really funny.' Dr. Messenger started to laugh, and Michael started to laugh again. They could not stop laughing. They thought it was the funniest thing they could image, people being consumed by fire from heaven.

"Dr. Messenger said they were very lucky that Michael perfected the sound gun. 'But the real luck was when you were able to combine the sound with the chemical solution that ignites into a fire ball when it enters the earth's atmosphere.'

"Michael stated, 'The real luck was when Dr. Wilson gave me the idea of a satellite that shot fire balls from heaven. '

"Dr. Messenger said, 'Since we will have all the religions under one umbrella, we need to have an office in Jerusalem and New York. With Jerusalem becoming an international city, visitors will want to have a place to worship. We need to build or we need to buy a church building.'

"Michael said, 'Don't forget Rome.'

" 'Rome,' Dr. Messenger said, 'how could anyone forget Rome?'

"When Dr. Messenger made the comment, "How could anyone forget Rome,' he was really being sarcastic. The statement he made about all religions coming to Babylon was not accepted by the Pope. The headquarters of the Roman Catholic Church had been in Rome for hundreds of years. For the headquarters to be moved to Babylon was unthinkable. The Pope was old; it would only be a very short time before he would die. But Dr. Messenger and Michael decided they should help the old man along the way, just a little. One person who was a loyal follower of the new religion was one of the Cardinals in Rome. The Pope had his cup of tea every night. The Cardinal who normally served the Pope his tea was killed in an accidental car wreck. When Michael and Dr. Messenger decided to have someone removed, it was always an accident. So the new person chosen to give the tea to the Pope was the Cardinal who was one of Dr. Messenger's followers. As was the custom of the Pope, every night he had his cup of tea. Each night there was a small amount of poison added to the tea. Within two weeks the Pope was gone.

"With the Pope gone, there had to be a new leader of the Catholic Church elected. Since all the religions were located in Babylon, the new head should be someone that was known world-wide. There was only one person who could be elected, and that would be Dr. Messenger. It was voted on, and the new head of the Catholic Church would be Dr. Messenger. Since all religions believed the same thing and the soon coming of god would take place within 3-1/2 years, Dr. Messenger would be god's right hand man. Soon all the other religions of the world thought it would be best to have Dr. Messenger to be their head also. One month after Michael signed the peace treaty, Dr. Messenger became the head religious leader of all religions of the world. He was what the Bible called the False Prophet.

"I said Dr. Messenger despised Dr. Mohammed. Many times they would have heated exchanges about the direction of the church. One day they were talking about the different things that should be changed, and Dr. Mohammed stated there would be no changes unless he made that decision. Dr. Messenger tried to smooth the feathers of Dr. Mohammed, but Dr. Mohammed knew exactly what Dr. Messenger was trying to do. 'We believe all people of the world must come and worship one god. They must convert to our religion or they will not be accepted.' Dr. Messenger said people would not convert to his religion. They would not leave their own religion for a new religion that was headed up by someone who was hard headed. 'I may be hardheaded, but I will not let anyone join my church unless they reject what they have been involved in.' Those two men were having disagreements almost every day. There had to be a change, and the change came upon the death of Dr. Mohammed.

"When Dr. Messenger started making the changes, he knew the new religion had to be in every country of the world. With his friends in high positions in every country, he was able to have all the other religions outlawed. Some countries outlawed one religion after another, while other countries outlawed all religions at once. The only religion that was open for worship was the 'Fellowship of World Believers.' Most countries imposed strict penalties for those who broke the law. If you were caught worshipping any other religion, you were given a mandatory five-year prison sentence. There was only one thing a person could do if he wanted to worship other religions. They could go to Jerusalem. Not only was Jerusalem an International City, but one could worship any religion they wanted there. Dr. Messenger knew he could not outlaw other religions in Jerusalem as long as there was the Jewish religion. If he did not want a war, the Arabs could worship any religion they wanted, also. All of that would change in a very short period of time.

"Dr. Messenger made a statement that most people believed was the most important statement he ever made. In every country in the world, on Sunday he had a radio program which was titled, 'Preaching to the Believers.' He gave a one-hour sermon on the beliefs of the only true religion in the world. On one particular Sunday, his sermon was on, 'How Can a Person Know He Is Secure?' He started his sermon with many of the things he had said before, but then he said, 'Just like in Christianity where they believe they have eternal security, our religion can prove we are secure. Eternal security starts in the mind, and it goes out in all directions. The different directions it goes and the result it brings back is called WORKS. If Christianity was the true religion in the world, then the eternal security they believed in would have reached the entire world and brought back great WORKS. But did they reach the whole world, and if they did why did their WORKS not show it? One can see our great WORKS by our faith. We have reached the whole world with our religion, and the whole world has responded.

This proves beyond a shadow of a doubt that we have secured our faith by our WORKS.'

"When he would finish his sermons, everyone would stand up and applaud, but not this Sunday. Everyone stood and did not applaud or say anything; they just stood there, speechless. It was his custom to walk to the back and greet everyone as they left. On his way to the back, he was wondering what he had said that made everyone mad. He had never seen people act like this before. What would he say as they left, or maybe it was best if he said nothing and let the people do all the talking. As he walked to the back, he could sense all eyes following him. Each step he took, he was aware of their piercing eyes.

"When the first person walked out and shook his hand, he said it was the most profound sermon he had ever heard. 'It was unlike any other sermon you have ever preached. It seemed to come from the heart other than the mind.' One person after another said the same thing as they left.

"The next day in the newspaper and all over the news were comments about the greatest sermon ever preached. Dr. Messenger could not believe the response he was receiving. When questioned about the sermon, he said he and Michael had talked about different topics he should speak about. 'Michael suggested the topic and also helped write more than half of the sermon. Michael should be the one who receives the credit for the sermon. Without his help, I would not have achieved the clear teaching on the believer being secure.'

"Dr. Messenger decided every Sunday he could give another great sermon. The sermon on eternal security was twisted just a bit, but the result was astounding. He decided to take other doctrines from the Bible and just give them a little twist also. He took the doctrine of the Shed Blood of Christ and wrote a sermon he thought the people would like. He stated that when Neanias comes, he must cleanse the world. 'The only way to cleanse the world is for god to give his blood for the world. Neanias will give his own blood for the whole world.' After the sermon, Michael asked Dr. Messenger how he, 'Michael,' was going to shed his blood for the world. Dr. Messenger said, 'We have 3-1/2 years to put together a plan the world will accept." Doctrine after doctrine was counterfeited and twisted to meet the needs of Dr. Messenger. Dr. Messenger was a liar and a very good one at that. He could take any verse in the Bible and twist it to mean anything he wanted.

"At this time, I will take any questions you may want to ask."

"Why did Dr. Messenger give a sermon on the believer being secure?"

" Well, as we all know, the believers he was referring to were those in the false church. Dr. Messenger knew how the Christians enjoyed hearing sermons on the great doctrines of the Bible, so he decided to twist the doctrine of eternal security. He probably thought this would be an easy one to begin with. He changed the meaning and the people the Bible was talking about. The first thing I must do is to teach you what eternal security truly is and what it is not. Most of you do not know what eternal security means. In order for you to understand what eternal security is, I will use an illustration. The people who became Christians during the tribulation and went into the millennium are saved for eternity. They cannot be lost. God has placed a seal upon them, and if they have been sealed they have eternal security. A person who has eternal security cannot be lost, period.

"One movement that caught fire during the last 50 years before the rapture was eternal insecurity. What that means is if a person were to sin and they did not ask for forgiveness immediately, and they were killed, they would go to hell. Some churches even taught that if you sinned you were not a Christian, and you would have to ask Christ to be your Savior all over again. In other words, one would have to crucify Christ a second or third or fourth time. The Bible says one salvation and one crucifixion. The majority of the people who believed in eternal insecurity did not understand what Christ did on the cross for them. They did not understand once you become a Christian, you are not sinless, you would still sin. They thought it was their salvation they lost, instead of losing rewards at the Bema Seat.

I guess you could say that most people were ignorant of the Word of God. They believed what their parents would tell them, or what their pastor would say, but to go to the Bible and check it out for themselves, that was something they never did. That was the main reason there was a falling away in the last days. People did not study the Bible. In First Corinthians 12:13, it says we were all placed into the body, that being the body of Christ. And in Ephesians 1:13, it says once we believe in Christ, we Christians are sealed. If we Christians were sealed before the rapture, then the idea of eternal insecurity is a lie that the devil made up to hold Christians in bondage. And he did a really good job of that. Churches would even put insecurity in their statement of faith. What a sad state the churches were in! They would take the statement of Christ when he said, 'If you believe in Me you have eternal life,' and say that Christ really did not mean what he said. What is the next question?"

"You make it sound as if everyone in the world were unbelievers. Were there any believers?"

"Yes, when the Antichrist signed the peace treaty, there were 144,000 Jews who believed that Jesus was the promised Messiah. Throughout the first half of the tribulation period, they spread the gospel to every part of the world. There were multitudes that heard the gospel and accepted Christ. In the late 1990s, there were an estimated 30,000 missionaries in the world. During the first half of the tribulation, those 144,000 Jews were all missionaries. These 144,000 had been sealed by Christ. What that meant was the Antichrist or the False Prophet could not harm them or kill any of the 144,000. I will take one last question."

"Brother Steven, I know you have told us before what makes Christ's blood different than our blood, but there may be some who did not understand. Could you explain it one more time?"

"This was one of the great doctrines during the Church Age. Sermon after sermon was preached on the sinlessness of Christ. You must remember sin came into the world because of what Adam and Eve did in the garden. They were forced out of the Garden of Eden and forbidden to ever enter the Garden again. The blood of Adam was sinful, and when they began to have children, that sinful blood was passed down from generation to generation. Every person born had the sinful blood given to them by their father. In Matthew 1:23 it says, 'Behold, the virgin shall be with child, and shall bring forth a son, and they shall call his name Immanuel, which, being interpreted, is God with us.' A virgin is a woman that has never had a sexual relationship with a man. So for Mary to have a child while she was a virgin was a miracle. If she would have had sexual relations with a man, her son would have the same sin nature that all men have. But Luke 1:35 says, 'And the angel answered, and said unto her, The Holy Spirit shall come upon thee, and the power of the Highest shall overshadow thee; therefore also that holy thing which shall be born of thee shall be called the Son of God.' The child who was born to Mary did not have the sinful blood that everyone else has. That child, Jesus Christ, did not have an earthly father. Remember, the only way sinful blood can be passed down is through the father. Since Jesus did not have an earthly father, he did not have the sinful blood. Since he did not have sinful blood, he was the only possible person to take the sins of the world upon himself, who had no sin of his own. That is why John the Baptist said in John 1:29 - 'Behold the Lamb of God, who taketh away the sin of the world.' I hope that answers your question. Tomorrow I will tell you about Michael moving the ECU headquarters to Rome."

CHAPTER 17

"**ISRAEL AND** the Arab nations would sign the peace treaty that would start the tribulation. However, Michael decided it was best to make one major change before he signed it. He decided the headquarters of the ECU should be moved to Rome. 'Since this is the revived Roman Empire, the headquarters should be where the capital was originally, over 2,000 years ago,' he reasoned aloud. Michael had already purchased land and his new building would be finished in three months. Instead of his corporation moving into the new building, he would sell it to the ECU. He also thought it would be best if there were branch offices set up in every major city in Europe and in the other countries that were backers of the ECU. The branch offices could move into any office space they could find. The first thing he would have to do was to have his plan passed by the 11 members of the ECU. He knew three members would vote no on anything that he proposed. But it did not make any difference; he would make a motion for the plan and let the delegates vote.

"Michael and Dr. Messenger knew they had to replace the three members who continued to vote no on any item that Michael brought up.

"The plan that Michael and Dr. Messenger liked was really sophisticated; no one would ever know or suspect it was murder. Nicholas Brassen was one delegate who did not like Michael. It did not make any difference if the idea would help his country or not, he would vote no if it was Michael's idea. Every summer his family would take a vacation to the warm waters of the Indo-Pacific area. Michael and Dr. Messenger decided the summer of 2011 would be his last summer. The plan was very simple. Michael would send four men to the area where Nicholas would be scuba diving. They would catch a stone fish and wait until Nicholas was diving alone. When people dive alone, sometimes things happen that cost them their lives. That would be the case with Nicholas. Three of the men would hold Nicholas while the other man would force the dorsal fin of the stone fish into him. The venom would be injected into Nicholas, and before he could make it to the surface he would die. The autopsy would indicate the poison came from a stone fish. The conclusion on the death certificate would state accidental. In Michael and Dr. Messenger's mind, it was the perfect crime. One plan down or, as they said, one delegate down and two to go. The other two plans would have to be something that no one had ever thought of before. All three plans would happen within a two-week period. The men that Michael was grooming to take the place of the deceased delegates would guarantee 11 yes votes on anything Michael proposed.

"While Michael and Dr. Messenger were thinking of two other plans, they continued to work on the move of the headquarters of the ECU to Rome. By having eight delegates always voting yes, he knew they would accept his proposal to buy his new building for the new headquarters. The ECU always went with the majority vote. The new building was designed by Michael. Each room had hidden cameras and microphones that could hear a pin drop. There were also hidden chambers and some rooms were soundproof. Michael had thought of everything. There was no way anyone could do anything without him knowing it.

"He had wondered many times previously why he had purchased the land and started building a 12-story building. Dr. Messenger also asked Michael the same thing many times, but Michael always said things would work out, just wait and see. Things did work out, just as Michael had said they would.

"The decision was made to leave a branch office in Brussels, and the most likely place for a branch office was the ex-headquarters of the ECU. If things were to change, they could always move the headquarters back to Brussels. Michael knew he had to have a branch office in every country that was a member of the ECU. So the first step was to have each delegate find a place that they thought would be suitable for a branch office. If Michael did not like the location, he would tell them in a way they thought they were being praised instead of being reprimanded or insulted.

"Michael said things in a way that made you feel good about yourself. He was very polite and never had a harsh word for anyone. Even though he never said anything derogatory out loud, he always thought everyone was stupid or they were dumb. He never tried to show how smart he was, but people could tell there was something different about him. He had a lot of head knowledge and used common sense to its utmost.

"Dr. Messenger came into Michael's office and said, 'I just came up with a plan that will make it possible for the second delegate to be murdered.' Michael was excited and wanted to know all the details. 'This is the way the plan goes. We have to use the headquarters in Brussels until the building in Rome is completed. So when Alex goes into the steam room, we make sure someone puts a drug in his drink. The drug must be one which cannot be traced by an autopsy. Once he is in the steam room, he will pass out and the steam can be turned up. With the room temperature soaring, it won't take much time for him to expire.'

"Michael looked at Dr. Messenger and said, 'I like the way you use words. You could have said he died or he suffocated, but to expire, that shows class.'

"Dr. Messenger winked at Michael and said, 'Sometimes we have to show a little class or we would not be who we are.'

"Michael agreed and said, 'Two plans down and only one to go.'

"The branch office in Jerusalem had to be completely different from the other branch offices. Jerusalem was going to be an International City, and that meant the office had to be a very plush office. Several things it definitely needed were the cameras and hidden microphones in every room.

"Michael told Dr. Messenger, 'We can't let people say anything and then let them get away with it. In the secret conference rooms, there will be a number of cameras and microphones. When there are meetings in Jerusalem, the different groups can go into a secret conference room that is soundproof. The cameras and microphones cannot be detected by scanning devices or other types of detection devices. When a group wants to have secret meeting, they will, of course, first scan the room for any bugs, such as microphones or cameras. Since their devices will indicate the room is clean, they will then meet and discuss their plans. We will know exactly what is said, and most of the time we can watch the whole meeting.' During the tribulation people would pay with their lives if they made statements that Michael or Dr. Messenger did not like. This was just the beginning of the lack of privacy and spying which would take place.

"Michael had made plans for Tom and Debbie also. He informed them that half of the time he would be in Rome and half of the time he would be in Jerusalem. He wanted them to be with him all the time. He said, 'Since there was an attempt to kill me in Rome right after the disappearance, I want you two to be with me so I can provide you with protection. Even though I was not in Rome, if I had not tripled the security around my mansion, you would have been killed.'

"Tom knew all about the cameras and microphones Michael and Dr. Messenger had installed in the buildings, but was not aware of any of those things in Michael's mansion. However, when Tom and Debbie wanted to talk, they were cautious and would take a walk or they would go into the freezer. Tom told Debbie, 'Michael does not know that we are Christians, but if he finds out, I know he will make examples of us to the rest of the world.'

"Debbie wanted to know what he meant when he said 'examples to the rest of the world'?

"Tom said, 'Since we are so close to Michael, if he finds out we are Christians, he will show the world that he has no compassion on people like us. The death that we would suffer would be an example to those that proclaim to be Christians.'

"Debbie wanted to know what Tom wanted to do. 'Shall we go hide in the closet or hide in the basement?'

"Tom said, 'No, we will live like we have always lived, but we will tell people about Christ and try to get as many saved as we can. If we do not make it completely through the seven years, that's fine, we have lived a long life. I just wish we would have become Christians early in life instead of waiting as long as we did.'

"Debbie had a little tear trickling down her cheek and said, 'I wish we would have accepted early in life also.'

"Tom asked Michael if he had any set schedule for the times he would be in Rome and when he would be in Jerusalem. Michael told him, 'No, most of the time something will come up and I will have to go to Rome or Jerusalem immediately. When that happens, I will leave a message telling you where I am. I know the media will want to know who you are and why are you always with me, so I think it is best to tell them that you are friends from the United States.'

"Tom wanted to know, 'Will we be living at the branch office in Jerusalem or somewhere else?'

" 'There is more protection at the branch office, but it is not like a home. I have been looking for a mansion in Jerusalem that could be protected from any attempts of terrorists. Once I find what I am looking for, that is where we will live. While in Rome we will continue to live at my mansion.' Michael had begun to make all the decisions for his benefit and, again, was not considering what anyone else might want or desire.

"Michael had to go to the United States for some very important meetings with the acting, 'soon-to-be President.' The first thing they discussed was a branch office in New York and one in Washington, D.C. He told the President, 'There will be some kind of military engagement in the near future, I'm sure. The U.S. must be ready when the call comes to launch nuclear weapons against our enemies. Also, it may be necessary for troops to be air lifted straight into battle.'

"The President asked, 'Do you know specifically of some trouble that you are not sharing with me?'

"Michael said, 'There is no trouble now, but I know the Russians are looking at Israel. When Israel destroys their weapons of war, the Russians will most likely make their move into the Middle East. I know that just as certain as I am standing here, the Russians will invade Israel.'

"The President wanted to know, 'Why don't we hit them with a surprise attack and destroy the country now?'

"Michael stated, 'I will be the savior of Israel. When Russia attacks, no other country will come to the aid of Israel. But I will rain down hail stones that weigh 100 pounds each upon the Northern Confederacy troops.'

"The President was bewildered by Michael's statement. 'How can you bring hail stones down upon the troops of the Northern Confederacy?'

"Michael said, 'I cannot say at this time, but you will see the power I have in the coming future. What I am telling you is that World War Three will be fought over Israel. However, the invasion of Israel by Russia is not the military action I was thinking about. I will not have to use any troops to defeat the Russians. But the engagements after that war will take a lot of troops. We must be ready when the time comes, and the time will come soon.'

"The next day the President reinstated the draft. All men under the age of 40 would have to sign up on a list in case there was a need for troops. The President informed the nation that most of those who would be drafted would be under 25, but they still needed to know how many men were under 40. Since the men who would be drafted would be under 25, the rest of the men, those over 25, would have to have 30 days of training a year, just in case things in the world started to heat up and they were needed. The President was not a very popular person, but since the disappearance of millions all over the world, people were thinking that maybe the aliens would come back. If they did, the U.S. would be ready.

"While in the U.S., Michael was watching one of the old movies that had been made in the seventies. The movie was 'The Godfather.' Michael was intrigued by the movie and the lifestyle of the character in the movie, Michael Coroleon. As he watched the movie, the more he was determined to eliminate the last delegate the same way that Michael in the movie would have it done. He would contract for a hit man. Michael wanted the last delegate to die knowing it was he, Michael Glispbe, who had contracted his murder. Michael purposed that he would have the movie, 'The Godfather,' sent to Ramon Garcia. Before Ramon was killed, there would be a telephone call to his house and the caller would ask if he had watched the movie. If he answered yes, the next day the hit man would approach Ramon and tell him, 'Remember the movie, 'The Godfather,' and the character Michael? This is from Michael.' At that time, the hit man would pull a pistol and kill Ramon. It would happen just like it did in the movies.

"Michael thought to himself, 'I sure do come up with many clever ways to remove those who oppose me. I must say, I surprise myself sometimes by my brilliance.'

"I know there are a number of questions that everyone wants to ask, so I will take as many questions as I can answer in the next one hour. I believe Wes wants to know how Michael knew about the Russian invasion of Israel. That is an easy question to answer. I told Michael about the invasion. One evening when Michael came over to my house, he asked if there were any major wars during the tribulation? I said in Ezekiel 38 and 39, the Russians are called Gog, of the land of Magog. We know the Russians are the ones spoken of in that verse because it speaks about the chief prince of Meshech and Tubal. The city of Moscow was named after Meshech, and Tobolsk was named after Tubal. When the Russians invade, there will be no countries in the world that will come to the aid of Israel. I told Michael how God will rain down hail stones that weigh 100 pounds upon the invading armies. The destruction by the hail stones will be so great, in 39:2, it says only one-sixth of the invading troops will escape. There is more than just one army in the battle. In 38:5 and 6 there are at least five other armies that go with Russia for the invasion. I had also told Michael about the coming Battle of Armageddon. When Michael told the President of the United States to be ready when he called upon him for military help, Michael was thinking about Armageddon.

"The next question is from Andy."

"I want to know why Michael said that he would rain down hail from heaven upon the invading armies?"

"Like I said, I told Michael about the invasion and about God destroying the invaders. I also made it very clear that there would not be any country coming to the aid of Israel. God would be Israel's savior. What Michael did was to try and take the credit for what God did against the Russian invasion. The world would believe it was Michael who saved Israel from certain destruction. The world had seen Michael call fire down from heaven and consume his enemies once before, and now they believed he had called hail down to destroy the Russian army and its allies. Who could fight against someone with that kind of power?"

"When Tom and Debbie were away from Michael, how did they witness for Christ?"

"Right after the rapture, Tom and Debbie flew to Rome so Michael could protect them. While in Rome and in Jerusalem, they became friends with many people. Some of the people recognized them from the commercials, while others they met and saw for the first time became friends. During their talks, people wanted to know about the disappearance and what was going to happen in the future. Tom shared with them the things that would soon happen and that Christ was the only way to live eternally. When Michael signed the peace treaty which began the tribulation, Tom and Debbie had to be very careful how and when they witnessed to strangers. During the first 3-1/2 years, they were able to lead many souls to Christ, but during the last 3-1/2 years they never realized how many people's souls would be saved simply by their actions and what they said. One last question and then I have to go."

"Did the cameras and microphones really catch people saying things that made Michael and Dr. Messenger mad?"

"The answer is yes. As a matter of fact, those who made Michael or Dr. Messenger mad were taken away and executed immediately. Also, when different delegates would meet and discuss different issues, Michael would watch and listen and then work up a plan before he met with the delegates. When he would walk into the room, he would say he had just come up with a new plan. The delegates would listen to the plan, and they would all be dumbfounded. The very thing they had just been talking about was solved by Michael."

CHAPTER 18

"THE ECONOMY of the world was in shambles. Michael had spent so much time working out the peace treaty and moving the headquarters of the ECU to Rome he had totally forgotten about other things. What would he do to get the world back to where it was before? When the rapture occurred, everyone believed the story Dr. Messenger had his friends circulate. 'Aliens from outer space came and took those known as the undesirables off the face of the earth.' But as the days came and went, the story of the rapture was more believable. The things the Bible had predicted were pointing to a thing called the Rapture, and the Bible had not missed a prediction yet. Still there were those who called it a fairy tale or something someone made up late at night. To believe there was a God and he was now ready to judge the world was absurd. The economy reflected the different ideas of the world. One day the rumors would be that it was the Rapture, and the banks would have a run on the money. The next day people would believe the lies told them and they would stop taking their money out of banks. The problem the banks were experiencing was that people would take money out but they never put money back into the bank. The banking business was the only area that Michael could not control. It was looking as if the world economy depended on the banks of the world.

"How much longer could the economy last? It could

collapse overnight, and if that were to happen it could make things worse than was planned. At this point in time, Michael or Dr. Messenger had no plans to pull the economy out of the mess it was in. The peace treaty that was going to be signed might bring stability. However, one rumor led to another until the run on the banks could not be stopped. People wanted their money, and they wanted their money now. Michael decided he had to do something to change the tide of despair. He informed all the TV networks he wanted to make a personal appeal to the world. At 6 p.m. Jerusalem time on April 1, he would address the world. He started out recapping the events since February 17. He said, 'We are now facing a crisis world wide that has to be stopped. I am requesting all banks, world-wide, to close for four days. Dr. Messenger, the officials of the ECU and myself are putting together a plan that will astound the world. The plan will bring world-wide stability back to the economy. We need time, we need for every person in the world to be patient. Your money is safe in the banks. If you want all your money or just a small amount of your money, in four days, that will be fine. But it is best to see how the new plan will work before you make any decisions.'

"The next day, all the banks in the world were closed for four days. After the newscast, Dr. Messenger asked Michael, 'What plan are you working on?'

"Michael said, "I don't have any plan, we needed time, so I bought us four days. In four days we had better come up with something that will work.'

"Michael had so many things going on at one time, he did not know which way to turn. On the third was the peace signing, the fourth was the world-wide commission of Dr. Messenger, and on the fifth he had to give the world a plan that would work for the economy. Plus, he was involved in moving the headquarters from Brussels to Rome. He decided the best thing to do was nothing. If he could just sit and do nothing but think, he felt he could come up with a plan that would work. He thought back to his grandmother and wondered what she would do or suggest. That was the key, his grandmother. She would say, 'The Jews have all the answers, why not ask one of them?'

"Michael called his friend, Barry Cohen, and asked for his uncle's telephone number. He called and they had a long talk about other diggings and how he was feeling and just chit-chat. Michael then asked for his idea about the economy. Barry's uncle said, 'If I were in charge, I would go back to the Old Testament way of doing business. Every 50 years, Israel had a jubilee year.' Michael wanted to know all about the jubilee year. He was told, 'All debts were done away with every 50 years. It did not make any difference how much money you owed, your bill was wiped clean. If the world had a jubilee year and all debts were wiped clean, the economy could not collapse.' The more Michael thought about a jubilee year, the more he liked it. He talked to Dr. Messenger and told him about the year of jubilee, and Dr. Messenger liked the idea also.

"There would be a six-point plan given to the world to ensure economic stability. The first point would be to celebrate 2011 as the year of jubilee. All debts would be wiped clean. All countries that owed money to other countries would not owe anything as of April 6. Any person in the world who owed money would be debt-free also. Dr. Messenger reluctantly stated, 'I don't think letting people off the hook is a very good idea.'

"Michael said with excitement in his voice, 'Let me explain. Since all debts are done away with, the world is debt-free. We must have one currency for exchange throughout the world. The ECU dollar will be the worldwide currency. All countries and all people still have money. What are they going to do with the money? All countries would have to buy the ECU dollar. The exchange will be one ECU dollar for every three dollars from a foreign country. Once we start the exchange, the ECU could buy their goods or other things with their traded money. They would take the ECU dollar and make the same exchange with their countrymen. We could print as much money as we wanted in order to keep the exchange going all year. During the first year, we will accept their dollar exchange. But in 2012, the only exchange will be the ECU dollar.'

"Dr. Messenger said, 'I still do not think it will work. The ECU will have all those worthless currencies from all over the world.'

" 'No, the ECU will not have worthless currencies. After the first year, every nation has to use the ECU dollar, but as long as we have other countries' currencies, we can use their money for goods or other things the ECU needs. All the countries will get their money back, which after the first year they will have to destroy. We own the printing presses. We can print as much money as we want. Since our dollar will be the only currency in the world, we will be the richest men in the world. We could print billions of dollars for ourselves, who would know the difference? After the first year, we could trade for goods or gold or silver, maybe diamonds. The world will need our dollar, and we will be dictating to the world what we would trade for. Just think, if they do not want to use money, there is one thing they can still use ... the ICAN credit card.' The more Dr. Messenger thought about the idea, the more he thought it would work.

"Dr. Messenger said, 'We need to refine each point so the world will understand what we are going to do."

"Michael said, 'Point one is, 2011 will be celebrated as a year of jubilee. Point two, all debts, world-wide, are wiped clean. No country owes another country, and no person owes another person. Point three, the exchange will be one ECU dollar for three dollars from other countries. Point four, the exchange will continue until 2012. At that time, the ECU dollar will be the only currency that will be used world-wide, and the ECU will not accept the currency from other nations. Point five, the ECU may use the currency from other countries to buy goods or other items of trade until they have depleted that country's currency. Point six, if a country needs to borrow money from the ECU, the ECU will accept gold, silver, jewels or other items considered priceless, such as paintings.'

"Michael and Dr. Messenger sat back and looked at the six-point plan for the world. Michael said, 'It amazes me how things just seem to work out.'

"Dr. Messenger said, 'They don't just work out, we are the smartest men in the world. This plan could only have been thought up by us. No one else in the world could do what we have just done. And it only took 30 minutes to work out a plan for the world.'

"A day or two ago I said the banks were the only thing in the world that Michael did not control. Now he would be dictating policy to all the banks in the world. Michael looked at Dr. Messenger and said, 'In four days, we will control the world. It will be totally ours. But the economies of the world could still collapse before the four days are up.'

"Michael told Dr. Messenger, 'If the world can hold on for four more days, everything will work out.' Michael thought about how everything had worked out up to this point. 'There is nothing that can stop us. Destiny is our other partner.'

"Dr. Messenger looked at Michael and said, 'What do you mean by that statement?'

"Michael said, 'You know who we are and you know that we have been destined to this time in history. I remember how Dr. Wilson explained the things that would occur before the rapture and the things that would occur before the Antichrist signed the peace treaty. He said the Antichrist and the False Prophet would prepare the world so that some day they could control the world. He also said the person who will sign the peace treaty will be the Antichrist. The peace treaty is about to be signed. Israel will sign and the Arabs will sign; there is only one person who will sign who is not part of Israel or the Arabs. That one person is ME. The person who signs that peace treaty is the Antichrist. I am the Antichrist, and you are the False Prophet.' They both sat and looked at each other and said nothing.

"Dr. Messenger decided to speak, but Michael told him to keep quiet, he was thinking. They continued to just sit there for another 20 minutes, and then Michael started to smile and then he started to laugh. He looked at Dr. Messenger and said, 'I just figured out what we are going to do.'

"Dr. Messenger said, 'I like the idea and we know it will work because you said we were destined for this time in history. Tell me one more time what the plan is and how we can make it work.'

"Michael explained what Dr. Wilson had said about the number 666. If anyone took the number they would be doomed for eternity. 'If they know they will be doomed, they will not accept the number. So, we must make people believe they need the number. Remember the ICAN credit card? The people didn't really need the card, but we made them think they needed the card. The same will hold true for the number. We will make them think they need the number. We have made decisions that have us in a position that makes giving everyone the number a reality. Our credit card access code will have 666 for the first three numbers. The world religion has the lapel pen that marks them as followers. What we must do is to keep those things going for two or three years so people will get used to using them. I remember what Dr. Wilson said. He said 3-1/2 years after the peace treaty is signed, the Antichrist will go into the temple and proclaim himself to be God. You made the statement right after you were installed as the new head of the world church that god was going to come in the form of man. Why did you make that statement?'

"Dr. Messenger said, 'I was searching for things to say that would impress the officials, and that just came out.'

"Michael said, 'Don't you see? Your prediction has made it possible for me to be declared as god. Three and one-half years after I sign the peace treaty, I will walk into the temple and proclaim myself to be god. Since Dr. Wilson said we are going to be cast into hell, I think it is best for us to take as many people with us as possible. We certainly can't be lonely if there are multitudes with us. If I am god, I can do anything I want. I have a debt that has to be paid. The Jews have hated me all my life. I told them one day I would get even. After 3-1/2 years, I will go into the temple and break the peace treaty and declare all religions of the world as subversive. I know the Jews will not accept the ban and they will continue to worship their God. At that time, I will exterminate them off the face of the earth. If, which I do not believe, we go to hell, we will take all the Jews with us. And by killing all the Jews, we will be killing all of God's people. History will say that I was 10 times worse than Hitler. What Hitler did will be nothing compared to what I am going to do. I will beat God at the number of people I have following me compared to his followers.'

"Dr. Messenger said, 'We really are not as bad as you say we will be. We have not killed that many people yet.'

"Michael said, 'I believe there is a verse in the Bible that describes what will happen to both of us the very moment I sign the peace treaty. I don't remember where it is, but I think it says we shall be changed, in a moment, in the twinkling of an eye. The moment I sign the treaty, something is going to happen to both of us that will change our personalities.' They both stood there and looked at each other. A smile started to come on Dr. Messenger's face, and then a smile came on Michael's. The smiles became bigger, and then they both started to laugh. They were laughing hysterically.

"Michael said, 'Are you laughing at the same thing I am laughing at?'

"Dr. Messenger said, 'If you are thinking that the change may make us better than what we really are even now, then we are laughing at the same thing.'

"Michael said, 'The change will have to make us better than what we are, how can we be any worse than what we are now?'

"When the treaty was signed, they did get worse. They both became diabolical.

"The economy of the world was teetering on the edge of destruction. Anything could make it topple. Gold prices were falling so quickly, even gold could be worthless if the spiral did not stop. Silver had already gone below $1 an ounce. The price of diamonds and other jewels was tumbling about as fast as the price of gold. Michael and Dr. Messenger did not seem to be worried about the economy. They felt certain nothing was going to happen until the peace treaty was signed.

"The economy did stabilize on the second day the banks were closed. People started thinking that Michael had control of all the problems of the world and the banking problems would be resolved just like all the other problems the world had faced for the last five or six years. Michael knew the economy of the world would rebound after the treaty was signed. He would be in control of almost everything in the world, and what he was not in control of at that time he would control at the mid-point of the tribulation. Michael had been groomed by the devil for the last 12 years. He was now on the verge of fulfilling Bible prophecy. The things the Book of The Revelation taught and what Daniel predicted were only a short time away at this point. Those people who went through the tribulation would never forget how horrible the times were, and how they prayed for the coming of Christ.

"Michael contacted the Central Bank of Europe and informed them of the plans that would be taking place. He requested they start to print money as quickly as they possibly could. 'The demand for our dollar will be worldwide, and we must have enough so each country can begin with $100 million.' The Chairman of the Central Bank said he did not think they could print that much money in such a short period of time. 'If it means you have to keep the presses going 24 hours a day, then do it.' The Central Bank had three banks printing money, but to run 24 hours, that was unheard of. 'The money must be printed,' was Michael's reply. 'If the world is to survive, we have to supply the money so the people will be able to buy, sell and do anything that would continue their way of life.'

"The banks hired extra help and gave them a crash course on printing money. Michael did everything he could to encourage the employees to work as fast as they could. He even put an incentive program that would make everyone rich if they could fulfill the quota. There were a number of people that did steal money, but Michael did not care if money was stolen. The presses could print all they needed.

"Are there any questions about the things we have talked about this day?"

"Could you tell me why all the countries of the world would give in to the idea of only one currency in the world?"

"Yes. There are three reasons why the world would accept the idea of one currency. The first reason is that Michael had all the answers to the problems of the world. The world had never heard of a year of jubilee, but they liked the idea. Michael was going to sign a peace treaty with Israel and the Arab countries very soon, and his best friend, Dr. Messenger, was going to be commissioned as the holiest man on earth. There wasn't anyone who had all the answers except Michael. The second reason was the nations of the world would not have any debt whatsoever. By wiping out all debts, each nation would be starting fresh, economically speaking. Also, all the people in every country would be out of debt. Each country was thinking the same thing. If the people were free from debt, they would buy almost anything they wanted, which meant it would boost their weakened economies. The third reason the other countries went for the idea was the exchange method. The way Michael put it, they all believed they were coming out on the better end of the deal. In 2012, the only money that could be used was the ECU dollar. But in 2011, each country could trade three dollars for every one of the ECU dollars. Then the ECU could give that money back in order to get different types of import items. The way the other countries figured, 'If we give the ECU our dollar for theirs, then we get our money back when we trade for goods, we haven't lost a thing.' Well, like I said, in 2012, the only currency that could be used was the ECU dollar. That is when the countries of the world realized what had happened.

"Did Michael and Dr. Messenger steal any of the printed money?"

"Let me ask you a question. Can you keep a boy out of the candy jar if no one is around? I think you already know the answer. They stole more money than they knew how to spend. Michael and Dr. Messenger had many secret bank accounts in Swiss banks and all over the world. One of them was making a trip to Switzerland every two weeks. At one time during the tribulation, they both had more than $200 billion dollars in secret accounts and in real estate. Back in college, Michael said he would be the richest man in the world one day in the future, and he did become the richest man in the world."

"With the power Michael and Dr. Messenger had, why did they kill the three delegates? They could have put pressure on the three governments to have the men replaced. So why have them killed?"

"Michael and Dr. Messenger were murderers. Killing three men was nothing in their minds. If by killing three they could fulfill their desires, then killing was not so bad. You have to remember, during the tribulation, Michael was responsible for the deaths of half the population of the world. About three billion people. Also, Michael would try to exterminate the whole Jewish race. In Zechariah 13:8 and 9, it says that two out of every three Jews would be killed. Do you remember what Michael said about Hitler? He said, 'What Hitler did to the Jews was child's play compared to what I am going to do.' Hitler murdered 6 million Jews, but consider, if there were 60 million Jews on earth when the tribulation began, Michael murdered 40 million. Before the rapture, if you said the Antichrist was going to murder that many people, they thought you were crazy. They said no one could kill that many people without the world rising up against that person. Not only did the world not rise up against the Antichrist for killing the Jews, but the world thanked Michael for doing it. I will take one last question. "

"Sometimes when you tell us what Michael and Dr. Messenger said and did, it seems like they had a little sense of humor, is that true?"

"The answer is yes. However, their sense of humor was more like a morbid sense of humor. They enjoyed taking someone's life. The more complicated the method they could think up to take a person's life, the more they felt like they were in control. Many times in the tribulation, they would kill just for the fun of killing. They would talk about their method and laugh and make jokes about all the different ways that could be used. They were sick and their minds were sick. You have to remember, they were being led by the Devil, and at the mid-point of the tribulation, Michael was indwelt by the Devil."

CHAPTER 19

"AT THIS TIME, I would like to express my heart to everyone in my community. During the last three months I told you how I was saved and what happened the last 10 to 12 years before the rapture of the church. Also the events which occurred during the 45-day lull period before the tribulation. As I look out at each and every one of you, I wonder to myself why you won't acknowledge that you are sinners and accept Christ. I can't search your hearts and change them, that is something you must do. The things I have shared with you should be enough for you to open your eyes to the fact that you need to place your faith in Christ, but you still won't believe. One day in the coming future, it will be too late for you to accept. Why wait? Do it now and know that you have eternal life.

"When I first started telling you of the past, I told you how I was saved. I think back how I was before I was saved. I had a lot of pride and I did not believe I had to depend on anyone or anything. I know now if I would have died from the snake bite, I would be waiting for the Great White Throne Judgment just like all the other unsaved people from all the ages. My eyes were opened to the fact that there was nothing I could do to save myself. I had to depend on someone else, and that person was Jesus Christ.

"All the things that happened before the rapture were preparing the world for the tribulation. But more than that, the hearts of people would either become hardened and they would reject, or they would be softened and they would accept. No one knew when the rapture would occur, but the Christians knew it was very near. I never thought I would make it to 2001 without the rapture occurring. When 2010 came, I was even more surprised. Sometimes I thought the rapture would never occur in my lifetime, but I was mistaken.

"From the time that I had wondered if Michael was the Antichrist until the rapture, it was 10 years. In 10 years things moved so quickly it was impossible to keep up with them. But when you think about those 10 years, one might say things moved really slowly, I guess. From a day-to-day life aspect, one could not see the changes, but by looking back, the changes occurred really fast. I remember the beginning of the second year of school when Michael came to my house for supper. He asked me a number of questions about the end times. If you remember, I told him there were four areas he had to control. One of those areas would be credit cards. Before the year was out he and Dr. Messenger formed the ICAN credit card company. As I look back, the credit card company started off slowly, but within one year, it was making progress by leaps and bounds. That first year was the pivotal year for Michael and Dr. Messenger. But as I said, God was letting everything come together to prepare the world for the Antichrist to take over. For me to tell Michael how to put all the other credit card companies out of business was part of God's plan. God has a plan, and his plan for the Devil will occur at the end of this age.

"At the end of this age, the Devil will be let loose for a short period of time to deceive the nations. On a day-to-day basis, the change will not be seen, but if you could speed time up and go into the future, you could look back and see how fast the Devil deceived the world. The short 10 years that it took for Michael and Dr. Messenger to set everything up so they could take over the world was amazing. People did not realize what had happened until it was too late. The same thing holds true for each of you. We don't know how long the Devil will be loose upon the earth. It could be 20 years, or it could be 50 years. The Devil works very fast. When I think back to the Global Stock Exchange Michael set up, it does not seem possible all the other stock exchanges could be put out of business in a short period of time. The lies and the unscrupulous methods used by Michael and Dr. Messenger to attain their goals are what the Devil will use in the last days of the millennium. You are still 400 to 500 years away from the ending days of the millennium, but you can make a decision for eternity now. If you accept Christ now, you won't have to worry about that time when the Devil is let out of the bottomless pit.

"I know many of you do not believe there is a place called Hell and there is a being called the Devil. The reason you do not believe is because you have never been tempted. The Devil and all his demons are locked up and they cannot escape. There is a place called Hell and there is a great multitude of people that will be placed in that pit. Jesus tells us about the rich man and Lazarus. He also tells us of a place called hades. In hades there were two compartments. One compartment was called Paradise, and the other was called the Compartment of Torment. The compartment of Paradise does not exist because Christ took it with him when he went to heaven. The compartment of Torment is still very active. When a person dies and he is unsaved, he goes to the compartment of Torment. They are kept there until the final judgment. But I think it is best if I read what the Bible says about the compartment of Torment.

"Luke 16:19-31 says, *'There was a certain rich man, who was clothed in purple and fine linen, and fared sumptuously every day. And there was a certain beggar, named Lazarus, who was laid at his gate, full of sores, And desiring to be fed with the crumbs which fell from the rich man's table; moreover, the dogs came and licked his sores. And it came to pass that the beggar died, and was carried by the angels into Abraham's bosom; the man also died, and was buried; And in hades he lifted up his eyes, being in torments, and seeth Abraham afar off, and Lazarus in his bosom. And he cried and said, Father Abraham, have mercy on me, and send Lazarus, that he may dip the tip of his finger in water, and cool my tongue; for I am tormented in this flame. But Abraham said, Son, remember that thou in thy lifetime receivest thy good things, and likewise Lazarus evil things; but now he is comforted, and thou art tormented. And beside all this, between us and you there is a great gulf fixed, so that they who would pass from here to you cannot; neither can they pass to us, that would come from there. Then he said, I pray thee, therefore, father, that thou wouldest send him to my father's house; For I have five brethren that he may testify unto them, lest they also come into this place of torment. Abraham saith unto him, They have Moses and the prophets; let them hear them. And he said, Nay, father Abraham; but if one went unto them from the dead, they will repent. And he said unto him, If they hear not Moses and the prophets, neither will they be persuaded, though one rose from the dead.'*

"The compartment of Torment is a place where no one wants to go once they arrive. They would do anything if they could escape. They had a choice. They could have accepted Christ and have gone to heaven, or they could have rejected Christ and be tormented. Those people, before the millennium, had a choice. Many said, 'I don't believe in God' or they said they did not believe a loving God would put them in a place called Hell. God did not make that choice for them, just as God cannot make that choice for you. You will choose between rejecting or accepting Christ. Your choice determines where you will spend eternity. If you accept, you will have eternal life or everlasting life. If you reject, you will be placed in that compartment of torment until the Great White Throne Judgment. At the judgment, you will see every time you had a choice to accept or reject, and when the time comes for you to be placed in the pit of Hell, you cannot blame anyone but yourself for refusing to accept Christ.

Some people say they are not going to accept, but they are not going to reject either. They think they can walk the fence, and by not rejecting they will find that God is compassionate toward them. God is compassionate toward those who accept him. But for those who will not accept him, he will have no compassion. There is no in-between ground with God. You either accept or you reject. If you do not accept him, it is an automatic rejection of him.

"The way Dr. Messenger could take verses out of context and make them say anything he wanted them to say was astonishing. But the real master of taking verses out of context is the Devil. When he is let loose, he will use the same methods to deceive the world that he has used in the past. If the period of time is 30 or 40 years, he will lead people to an eternal hell. Many times in the last 350 years there have been many opportunities for you to accept Christ. Why not choose eternal life instead of eternal death? I could look in the Book of Life to see which of you are saved and which are lost, but I know I would be saddened if I knew the ones who are lost.

"Sometimes you remind me of Dr. Mohammed. He was a very religious man, but he was lost. When he set up his religion, he thought it was the most perfect religion in the world. He thought to himself how *he* had set it up and how *he* was preparing the world for the largest revival in the history of the world. His pride was blinding him to the fact that being religious does not save you. He had all the words that made a person believe he was a very holy man who knew God. At the Great White Throne Judgment, God will tell him, 'Depart from me, I never knew you.' Those of you out there who are not saved look just like the ones who are saved. I cannot tell the difference between one or the other. God knows the heart, and God knows which ones love him and which ones hate him. Dr. Mohammed loved the world and the things the world had to give. The most precious thing that God could give, Dr. Mohammed did not want; that is eternal life.

"If you remember, I told you how to pray to God if you were a sinner, and he would hear your prayers and you could become a Christian. Many of you did pray that prayer, but many of you did not. At this time, I will pray a prayer and if you say the words also and mean what you say, God will accept you and you will have eternal life.

"Lord, I know I am a sinner and I know there is nothing I can do to save myself. I want to accept you as my personal savior and know that I have eternal life. When the Devil is let out of the pit, I do not want to be tempted with sin, I want Jesus to come and live within me. Amen."

"At this time I want those who prayed that prayer with me to come up front and I will tell you how you can know that you have eternal life.

There were 87,000 people in the theater. I did not know how many people would come forward, but as they came I could not believe my eyes. There were 6,220 that came forward. I knew I could not tell each one about eternal life, so I asked for help from the Lord. In seconds, there was one immortal for each person who came forward. Each person was shown different scriptures that told about eternal life through Jesus Christ. The last verse the immortals used was John 3:16. For the next 600 years, those who came forward will not have to worry about being tempted by the Devil.

"Those of you who still have not made your choice, the Lord does still care about each and every one of you. You may not be saved but he still cares. He does not want any one of you to go to an eternal death. If you think back on the large fire in Jerusalem that I told you about, Michael had so much compassion on the children that were burned he invented artificial skin. The artificial skin was used so the burn victims would not have scars for the rest of their lives. The compassion the Lord has for you is far greater than the compassion shown by Michael. He has so much compassion He was willing to sacrifice His own Son for you. When Jesus died on the cross, he died for the world. But if you were the only person in the world, he would have died just for you. That is how much God cares for you. The only thing he asks is that you accept Him.

"As everyone knows we will be leaving for Jerusalem in three days to worship Christ at the temple. I will not have any more teaching sessions until we get back from Jerusalem. It is best if everyone prepares himself for the time of worshipping before we leave. Christ already knows how many people were saved this day, and

He is rejoicing with His angels. Those of you who accepted Christ this day should tell your loved ones and your friends what you did. It may be that they are not saved, and what you did today would be enough for them to want the same eternal life that you now have. No one is guaranteed another day on earth. It may be that this would be their last day on earth, and if they do not accept they will have but one place to go after the judgment. That place is Hell. If you care about your family and friends tell them, TELL THEM, PLEASE TELL THEM, PLEASE TELL THEM NOW! "

EPILOGUE

The peace treaty was signed on April 3, 2011, at 10 a.m. The world thought it had peace, but what it really had was the dreaded tribulation. The very moment the Antichrist, Michael Diabolos Glispbe, signed the peace treaty, 144,000 Jews accepted Jesus Christ as their personal Savior. For the next seven years, the 144,000 would spread the Gospel throughout the world. Multitudes of people would accept Christ as their personal Savior. Those people who accept will also spread the gospel throughout the world. When the Great Tribulation begins, the people who have been saved by the preaching of the 144,000 will pay with their lives for their faith in Jesus Christ.

Tom and Debbie spread the news of Christ's love to many people also. They tell more people than they can remember about how Christ died on the cross for their sins. Michael never knew about Tom and Debbie being Christians until the end of the tribulation. When they are caught giving out tracts, they know they will be killed. As Tom had told Debbie previously, "Michael will make examples of us." And that is exactly what Michael has in mind. He is going to show he has no compassion for those people who call themselves "Christians."

When Michael negotiated the peace treaty, one point he put in the treaty was for the guillotine to be used in Israel to execute terrorist and criminals. They would be put to be death in a public execution. The guillotine stopped terrorist acts and all forms of crime in Israel. The other nations throughout the world saw how crime was stopped in Israel, and they all decided to install the guillotine as their method of execution, also. Tom and Debbie know the guillotine is waiting for them.

When the Great Tribulation starts, Michael says everyone must have a mark in the right hand or in their forehead in order to buy, sell, or to hold a job. If anyone refuses to take the mark, he or she will have their head cut off, in a public execution. The mark Michael wants everyone to take is the number 666.

Michael and Dr. Messenger explain that taking the mark should be no big deal. Everyone in the true church has a lapel pen they wear to prove they are believers. Also, the first three numbers of Michael's access code are 666. "By taking the number, you are simply saying to everyone in the world that you believe Michael is the god, Neanias." Many things occur during the tribulation. God pours out judgment after judgment upon the world. The world is turned upside down. Men want to die, but it is impossible for people to commit suicide during the tribulation. War and famines take their toll on the people of the world. More than half the population of the world dies before the tribulation is over.

When Michael signed the peace treaty, he and Dr. Messenger were changed. They both became very diabolical. The Devil was the one calling the shots and dictating how they would change the world. At the midpoint of the tribulation, the Devil will indwell Michael, and he will rule the world with such cruelty no one in the history of the world can be compared to him. Michael lost his soul and will suffer spiritual death for eternity for his rejection.

The first 3-1/2 years of the tribulation are mild compared to the last 3-1/2 years of the tribulation. When Michael enters the tribulation temple and proclaims himself to be God, the Great Tribulation will begin. On the very day Michael enters the temple, the two prophets of God descend from heaven and begin their ministry. During their ministry they will shut up the heavens so it will not rain during the last half of the tribulation. It is impossible for anyone to kill them. If anyone tries to kill God's two prophets, fire will proceed out of their mouths and their enemies will be consumed where they stand.

Those people who had not accepted or had rejected Christ went into the tribulation. If they could have a second chance, they would choose to accept Christ and miss the tribulation.

What about you? You have a chance to miss the tribulation. Will you take it or will you reject it? IT IS UP TO YOU!

Join Tom and Debbie as they experience the tribulation and the suffering the world faces in
THE PAST OR THE COMING FUTURE PART II.